THE ART OF WOODWORKING

SHARPENING AND TOOL CARE

THE ART OF WOODWORKING

SHARPENING AND TOOL CARE

TIME-LIFE BOOKS
ALEXANDRIA, VIRGINIA

ST. REMY PRESS
MONTREAL • NEW YORK

THE ART OF WOODWORKING was produced by
ST. REMY PRESS

PUBLISHER	Kenneth Winchester
PRESIDENT	Pierre Léveillé
Series Editor	Pierre Home-Douglas
Series Art Director	Francine Lemieux
Senior Editor	Marc Cassini
Editor	Jim McRae
Art Directors	Normand Boudreault, Luc Germain
Designers	Hélène Dion, Michel Giguère
Picture Editor	Christopher Jackson
Writers	Andrew Jones, David Simon
Research Assistant	Bryan Quinn
Contributing Illustrators	Gilles Beauchemin, Roland Bergerat, Michel Blais, Jean-Guy Doiron, Ronald Durepos, Robert Paquet, Maryo Proulx, James Thérien
Administrator	Natalie Watanabe
Production Manager	Michelle Turbide
System Coordinator	Jean-Luc Roy
Photographer	Robert Chartier
Administrative Assistant	Dominique Gagné
Proofreader	Garet Markvoort
Indexer	Christine M. Jacobs

Time-Life Books is a division of Time Life Inc.,
a wholly owned subsidiary of
THE TIME INC. BOOK COMPANY

TIME-LIFE INC.

President and CEO	John M. Fahey
Editor-in-chief	John L. Papanek

TIME-LIFE BOOKS

President	John D. Hall
Vice-President, Director of Marketing	Nancy K. Jones
Executive Editor	Roberta Conlan
Executive Art Director	Ellen Robling
Consulting Editor	John R. Sullivan
Production Manager	Marlene Zack

THE CONSULTANTS

Mike Dunbar builds fine furniture at his workshop in Portsmouth, New Hampshire. The author of seven books and a contributing editor of *American Woodworker* and *Early American Life* magazines, Dunbar also offers Windsor chairmaking seminars across North America.

Giles Miller-Mead taught advanced cabinetmaking at Montreal technical schools for more than ten years. A native of New Zealand, he has worked as a restorer of antique furniture.

Ted Fuller is product manager at Delta International Machinery/Porter Cable (Canada). He is currently working in new product development and marketing for woodworking tools and equipment. He is also an amateur woodworker.

Sharpening & tool care.
    p. cm.— (The Art of woodworking)
Includes index.
ISBN 0-8094-9933-9
1. Woodworking tools— Maintenance and repair.
2. Sharpening of tools.   I. Time-Life Books.
II. Title: Sharpening and tool care.
III. Series.
 TT186.S45 1994
684'.08'028—dc20   94-26232
                                            CIP

For information about any Time-Life book,
please call 1-800-621-7026, or write:
Reader Information
Time-Life Customer Service
P.O. Box C-32068
Richmond, Virginia
23261-2068

CONTENTS

6 **INTRODUCTION**

12 **SHARPENING BASICS**
14 The cutting edge
16 Sharpening tools and accessories
18 Benchstones
20 Bench grinders

24 **SHARPENING AND MAIN-TAINING HAND TOOLS**
26 Handsaws
30 Chisels and gouges
39 Bench planes
46 Scrapers
51 Roughing and shaping tools
55 Braces and bits

58 **SHARPENING POWER TOOL BLADES AND BITS**
60 A gallery of blades and bits
61 Tools and accessories for sharpening
62 Router bits and shaper cutters
64 Molding knives
65 Drill bits
70 Circular saw blades
73 Band saw blades
79 Jointer and planer knives

86 **MAINTAINING PORTABLE POWER TOOLS**
88 Maintenance tips and schedules
90 Anatomy of a router
92 Anatomy of a saber saw
94 Anatomy of a plate joiner
95 Anatomy of an electric drill
96 Anatomy of a sander
97 Anatomy of a circular saw
98 Repairing portable power tools

104 **MAINTAINING STATIONARY POWER TOOLS**
106 Basic stationary tool maintenance
108 Table saws
113 Radial arm saws
120 Band saws
126 Jointers and planers
131 Drill presses
133 Lathes and shapers
136 Other tools

140 **GLOSSARY**

142 **INDEX**

144 **ACKNOWLEDGMENTS**

Richard Starr on the
VALUE OF SHARP TOOLS

When I was a kid I thought working wood was really difficult. It was, too, because my dad's tool bench was dominated by rough screwdrivers and assorted wrenches, dull saws, and a few auger bits. I remember it with fondness because it helped set me on my life's path, but it sure didn't encourage me to master the pieces of rough, splitty pine that I occasionally worked on.

Sharp hand tools were a revelation to a guy who grew up thinking that woodworking required some sort of special genius and a lot of powerful equipment. When I encountered a craftsman who built fine country furniture, miles from the nearest power line, I was inspired to learn as much as I could about how to make tools work well. As a result, wood became a much more welcoming material to me. Today, as a seasoned teacher of woodworking to children, my job is to help my students appreciate the possibilities of wood. The last thing I want to do is let them work with bum tools.

It is easy to fall in love with hand tools. I have a small collection of time-mellowed implements that I would not think of putting to work. They represent a history of effort and problem-solving that is a comfort to my modern mind. I also have other fine old tools that are frequently put into service. But the tools I use every day in teaching have much less of an aura about them. Kids bang them around and drop them all too frequently. What is important about them is that they work right.

The difference between a dull tool and a sharp one is something every woodworker needs to know. It is the difference between the frustrated kid I was and the kids I teach today. When I show a child how to whittle, he or she is expected to try every knife on the rack, usually four or five tools. Only by making this comparison will it become clear which are really sharp and which are just okay.

Every woodworker has his or her own preferred way to sharpen an edge tool. Some use oil stones, slow sandstone wheels, Arkansas stones or leather strops. Others prefer Japanese water stones, the use of which is almost a ritual. In my school shop, I need to work quickly and I have long since settled on a grinding belt and buffing wheel. At home, I have fallen in love with the new technology of diamond stones.

I firmly believe that, while sharp tools are essential, there is no one right way to sharpen tools, only the best way for you. It takes time to figure it out, but it is time you must be willing to spend. It is like building the foundation of your home. Everything else rests on it.

Richard Starr has taught woodworking to middle school students in Hanover, New Hampshire, since 1972. His book Woodworking with Kids *is published by Taunton Press. Starr has written numerous articles for* Fine Woodworking, Today's Woodworker *and other publications. His television series* Woodworking for Everyone *was broadcast on public television.*

Philip Lowe discusses

MAINTAINING POWER TOOLS

Stepping up to a poorly maintained machine can create a spectrum of emotions from apprehension to frustration. When the handwheel on your table saw forces you to one knee, requiring two hands and all of your strength to raise the blade, and when the machine screams and smoke billows as stock is fed through, face it: It's time to do a little maintenance!

Perhaps the most straightforward part of shop maintenance is the obvious reason behind it: safety and efficiency. It is very important to keep cutting implements sharp. More accidents occur with dull tools because more force is required to operate the tool.

You'll need a few tools to get you started, including a grease gun, an oil can, WD-40™, graphite, silicon spray, and paste wax. It is also convenient to have a set of wrenches, sockets, hex wrenches, and brushes for cleaning gears. Finally, pick up some abrasives such as steel wool, fine silicon carbide paper, and a mill file for deburring shafts and nicks in tabletops.

Cutters such as saw blades, knives for jointers and planers, shaper cutters, bits for routers and drill presses and turning tools must be kept sharp and free of pitch and resin in order to cut cleanly. Pitch and resin on cutters and saw blades, which can cause kickback, can be removed with spray oven cleaner. Some in-house sharpening can be done to carbide tools with a diamond stone. High-speed steel cutters such as turning tools and shaper knives can be sharpened on a bench grinder or honed with a bench and slip stones.

Alignment of tables and fences is also important. The position of a tabletop is important especially if it has slots cut in it for miter gauges. The slots need to be parallel to the cutters. The same is true for fences.

Lubricate gears and ways that raise and lower arbors and tables. Lubrication of exposed gears and ways should be done with graphite, spray silicon, or paste wax. These dry lubricants prevent build up of sawdust that would occur if the parts were greased or oiled. Bearings with grease fittings or oil caps should be attended to periodically with the appropriate lubricant.

The tables and beds of all machines should be inspected and, if necessary, filed flat. These surfaces should be kept free of rust and paint splatterings and should be cleaned with steel wool or fine silicon-carbide paper. Once clean, an application of paste wax will help prevent rust and allow stock to slide across the surface with less effort.

Philip C. Lowe makes fine furniture in his studio in Beverly, Massachusetts. Lowe has been building furniture for clients throughout North America for the past 25 years, and has spent 10 years as head instructor of the furniture program at North Bennet Street School in Boston, Massachusetts. He is affiliated with the Fine Woodworking *series of videos and his written works frequently appear in their magazine.*

Ian Waymark talks about

DIFFERENT WAYS TO SHARPEN

The old adage "Tools do not make the craftsman" contains a degree of truth. Still, sharp tools—although they will not make you a craftsperson—will greatly improve and enhance your skills. In fact, in my opinion, a great deal of skill displayed by today's craftspeople is based largely on their ability to create and maintain a keen edge on their cutting tools.

My wood turning travels throughout North America, Australia, and New Zealand have brought me in contact with many first-class woodworkers, carvers, wood turners, and just plain "hewers" of wood. They have worked in schools, home workshops, and craft fairs, with a variety of tools from the very best high-speed steel to the crudest home-made implements. Still, they all had one thing in common: They used sharp tools.

As varied as the crafts and craftspeople are, so are their methods and tools used for sharpening. Each one, used correctly, will create a keen cutting edge. The best are those that do not overheat cutting edges. This is probably the most common problem experienced by novices when sharpening tools. It is especially serious if the tool is made of carbon tool steel rather than high-speed steel. When carbon tool steel is heated until it turns blue the "temper" or "hardness" is removed, and the tool becomes soft and will not hold an edge for more than a few seconds. High-speed steel, on the other hand, will sustain a great deal of heat without damage.

The simple solution to "tip burning" is to use sharpening equipment that does not generate high heat or to use equipment that is constantly cooling the cutting edge as it is being ground. Wet grinding will assure the woodworker a cool cutting edge for two reasons: First, the grinding wheel is flooded with a coolant (usually water) to prevent heat buildup and second, the wet grinding wheels usually turn at a very slow rate which reduces the heat generated by the grinding process. Personally, I find the wet grinding system both too slow and too messy. My experience with wet grinding has been one of constantly cleaning the slurry of sawdust and water from the stone.

My preference for sharpening is a white aluminum oxide grinding wheel followed by a quick touch-up on an extra-fine neoprene honing wheel. I choose the aluminum oxide wheel simply because its porosity makes it a very cool grinding wheel compared to old gray stone or the standard sanding belts or discs. It is also very fast-cutting, thereby reducing the time at the grinder and reducing the time allowed for the heat to build up on the cutting edge. To hone my tools I use a neoprene wheel because it is fast and it maintains the hollow grind formed by the grinding wheel.

Ian Waymark has taught industrial education in Canada for 16 years. He is the owner of Woodturner's World, a store on Gabriola Island, British Columbia, that specializes in wood turning tools. Waymark designed the Orca 1 lathe and the Sabre Sharpening Center.

SHARPENING BASICS

At one time or another, virtually every woodworker has looked upon tool sharpening as a rainy-day task, an onerous duty undertaken only as a last resort that seems calculated to delay progress on the moment's favorite project. Although it may be impossible to persuade all woodworkers to embrace the joys of tool sharpening—as some do—sooner or later, most adopt an attitude of enlightened self interest, an understanding that regular attention to tool condition will speed, rather than retard, progress and improve both the quality of work and enjoyment of it.

In Japan, apprentice woodworkers spend years at the sharpening bench before attempting to cut wood. The practice is rooted in reality: To cut and finish wood, one must use sharp tools.

The most realistic route to sharp tools for most woodworkers lies in regular attention. When sharpening and maintenance are adopted as part of regular workshop routine, the time required is reduced—and the benefits of keen edges are quickly realized.

There are many jigs and accessories that promise quick and easy results, and no shortage of techniques with the same goal.

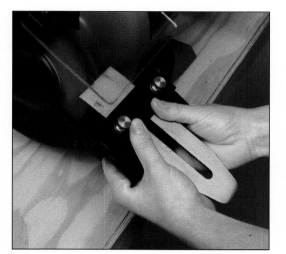

The nicked cutting edge of a plane blade is squared on a bench grinder. Clamping the blade in a commercial grinding jig keeps the end of the blade perpendicular to the grinder's abrasive wheel.

But all sharpening work comes down to this: Tools are sharpened by wearing away steel to form a fine edge, and polishing that edge so it slices as accurately and effortlessly as possible. Among many tools, two are essential: a sharpening stone and a grinder.

Once, all sharpening stones came from the ground; sandstone, novaculite, and other materials have been quarried and cut into bench stones *(page 18)* from the earliest days of woodworking. More recently, technology has produced synthetic stones that substitute for the dwindling supply of natural abrasives.

A somewhat older technology also provided the foot-powered sandstone grinding wheel and its descendant, the bench grinder *(page 20)*, which saves much labor in removing nicks and forming bevels before final honing.

This chapter is intended to remove the mystery and some of the labor from the sharpening process. With a grinder, a few benchstones, an understanding of the process *(page 14)*, and practice, you can have sharper tools—and derive more pleasure from your woodworking.

A Japanese finish stone is being used to polish the back of a butt chisel. Waterstones like the one shown at left are a good choice for putting the final polish on a blade. The fine abrasive slurry on the surface of the stone is formed by particles of abrasive and metal mixing with water.

THE CUTTING EDGE

A cutting edge can be defined as two flat, polished surfaces meeting at an angle. Since most blades are designed to be pushed through wood, a keen cutting edge is essential, particularly for dense hardwoods that can quickly blunt tools. Any flaw, like a nick in a planer knife or a chisel blade, will be transferred to the wood being cut.

Do not assume that just because a chisel is new that its edge is as sharp or as straight as it should be. Even the best tools need to be sharpened when new, and regularly thereafter. In order to achieve a keen cutting edge, steel is tempered to a certain hardness when the tool is forged. Since tempering is done at high temperatures, the tool may warp slightly as it cools. You can skirt this problem by choosing tools made with high-quality steel. Even the best steel is likely to show manufacturing imperfections. Low-quality tools, however, may never achieve and hold an edge.

In its simplest form, sharpening is like sanding: It consists of the wearing away of one material by a harder material, using successively finer abrasives. When the bevel of a chisel is drawn across a sharpening stone, the abrasive particles scratch the surface of the chisel uniformly, creating a flat surface. As shown below, finer and finer stones make the scratches finer and finer, until a mirror-like finish is achieved.

The difference between a dull and sharp cutting edge becomes obvious when a blade cuts into wood. On the left-hand side of the wood surface shown at left, a well-sharpened chisel severed the wood fibers cleanly, producing thin shavings; a dull chisel tore the wood fibers on the right-hand side of the board. Another way to determine whether a blade is sharp or dull is to examine the cutting edge itself; a dull edge reflects more light than a sharp one.

HOW SHARP IS SHARP?

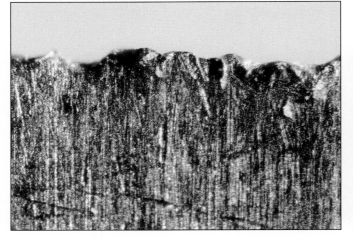

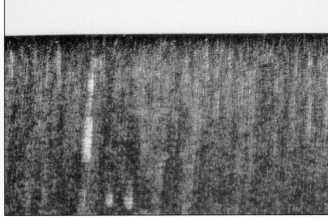

Smoothing a cutting edge

The quality of the cutting edge and finish on a tool blade depends on the size of abrasive particles used to sharpen it. Just as you would sand a tabletop with progressively finer grades of paper, sharpening begins with coarse abrasives and moves up through finer grits. The only difference is the size of abrasive particles involved. For example, a coarse India™ stone has particles measuring about 173 microns across, while a hard Arkansas oilstone has smaller particles—about 10 microns. Commerical honing compound used for buffing has extremely fine particles, as small as 0.5 micron. (By comparison, the diameter of a human hair is approximately 40 microns.) The photos above, of a chisel blade magnified approximately 200 times, reveal how sharpening improves a tool's edge. A dull chisel *(above, left)* has grooves and pits on its back and a nicked edge. These flaws will leave a rougher finish on wood than the smooth back and edge that is achieved after the chisel is sharpened and polished on a finish waterstone *(above, right)*. The waterstone has abrasive particles measuring 1 micron in diameter.

THE SHARPENING PROCESS STEP-BY-STEP

STEP 1: GRINDING OR LAPPING
For badly scratched or nicked cutting edges, start the process by squaring the cutting edge, grinding the bevel, then lapping or flattening the back of the blade. Grinding is done with a bench grinder and coarse stones such as Washita; lap with rough abrasives or lapping compounds on a lapping plate.

STEP 2: SHARPENING
For tools that do not need grinding, sharpening can start here. Initial sharpening removes any roughness on the bevel and establishes a fine wire burr on the back of the blade. Sharpening is done by hand or with bevel-setting jigs on medium stones such as soft Arkansas.

STEP 3: HONING
Honing uses progressively finer stones such as hard Arkansas or Japanese finishing stones to smooth out the scratches on the bevel caused by sharpening. Then the tool is turned over and lapped to remove the burr on the cutting edge. The microbevel *(below)* is also honed at this stage.

STEP 4: POLISHING
For a razor-sharp edge and a mirror-like finish, the tool can be polished with hard black Arkansas, ceramic or Japanese finish stones, as well as strops impregnated with fine buffing compounds.

BEVELS AND MICROBEVELS

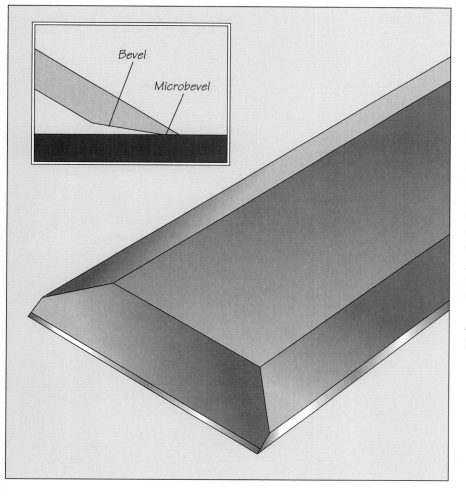

Bevel

Microbevel

Honing a microbevel
When a tool blade is razor-sharp, more force is necessary to drive the blade into the wood, and its edge is more likely to be brittle. By honing a secondary bevel, or microbevel, on top of the first *(inset)*, you can increase the cutting effectiveness of the tool and prolong the life of the cutting edge. Microbevels are slightly steeper than the original bevel of the tool. (For a list of common bevel angles for various blades, see the back endpaper of this book.) It can vary from as little as 2° to as much as 10°; the steeper the microbevel, the tougher the edge. Yet the microbevel should not be overworked. A few light strokes on a benchstone is usually sufficient to produce a small hairline strip at the edge of the main bevel *(left)*. If the microbevel is wider than half of the width of the bevel, the bevel should be reestablished by sharpening.

SHARPENING TOOLS AND ACCESSORIES

Honing compound
Applied to cloth wheel of grinder to polish sharpened bevel; contains a mixture of chromium dioxide and other fine abrasives

Benchstone (page 18)
Any oilstone or waterstone used to hone or sharpen tools

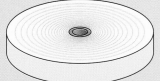

Neoprene polishing wheel
Rubber wheel for grinding and sharpening; available in grits between 90 and 240. Wheel must turn away from tool edge to prevent it from catching the edge

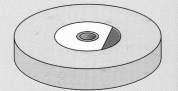

Aluminum oxide wheel
Standard wheel for grinding and sharpening; available in 6- and 8-inch sizes and a range of grits

Bench grinder (page 21)
Medium-grit wheel (left-hand side) squares and grinds blade; cloth wheel (right-hand side) polishes cutting edge

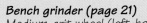

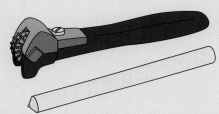

Dresser
Used to true or reshape grinder wheels and expose a fresh cutting surface. Star-wheel dresser (above) has up to four star-shaped wheels; diamond-point dresser (below) features a diamond set in a bronze tip

Felt wheel
Available in soft, medium, and hard; dressed with buffing compound for final polishing of cutting edge

Multi-tool jig
Skew-grinding jig (right, top) holds skews at 20° angle and pivots on center pin to grind radiused skew chisels. Sliding sharpening jig (right, middle) clamps tools under crossbar. Both are attached to an adjustable tool rest (right, bottom), which mounts to bench in front of grinder.

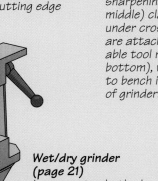

Wet/dry grinder (page 21)
Large, water-bathed wheel hones bevels; water prevents tools from overheating and carries away metal and grit. Smaller, dry wheel used for grinding

Lapping compounds
Set of silicone carbide powders used in conjunction with a lapping plate to flatten and polish tool backs; grits range from 90 to 600

Auger bit file
Used to sharpen auger bits and other drill bits; one end has no teeth on edges and other end has teeth only on edges to prevent filing adjacent surfaces

Single-cut bastard mill file
Used to sharpen spade bits and true the rims of Forstner bits

Cant-saw file
Used in place of a three-square file in openings of less than 60°

Three-square file
Triangular file used for sharpening Forstner and multi-spur bits

Sharpening stone holder
Secures oilstones and waterstones up to 8 inches long for sharpening; rubber feet hold stone in place

Angle checker
Brass guide for checking bevel and microbevel angles of sharpened tools; angles range from 15° to 120°

Honing guide and angle jig
For honing plane blades. Device holds blade at appropriate angle for honing a bevel; rotating the wheel on top of the jig sets angles between 15° and 35°

Diamond-coated honing files
Used to sharpen carbide router bits; stored inside their pivoting handles. Shown above from top: coarse, medium, and fine files

Strop
A leather strip glued to a handle; dressed with commercial honing compound or other fine abrasives to polish a sharpened edge

Diamond needle file
Small half-round file used for sharpening band-saw blades

Grit files
Boron-carbide stones used to sharpen router bits; gives a finer finish than diamond honing files of equal grit. Handle features magnifying lens for checking sharpness

Waterstone storage unit
Plastic reservoir used to immerse up to four waterstones for storage between sharpenings; features clamps that can be flipped up to hold the waterstone for sharpening or honing and a glass lapping plate

BENCHSTONES

The benchstone is the most commonly found sharpening accessory in the shop. Once referred to as natural stones, benchstones now encompass many man-made materials, ranging from aluminum oxide to ceramics. Many "stones" include fine diamond bonded to steel.

Sharpening stones are generally divided into two groups according to the lubricant used with them: oil and water. Lubrication serves to disperse ground particles and prevent them from clogging the stone. Choosing between the two is mostly a matter of feel; some woodworkers prefer the edge a glassy hard black Arkansas oilstone gives a tool; others like the fine control a softer Japanese finish waterstone offers.

Naturally occurring oilstones have long been regarded as the finest sharpening stones. Quarried from novaculite and sold as Washita and Arkansas stones, these sharpening surfaces are becoming scarce. If your budget permits, natural stones are a good investment; they will last a lifetime.

Synthetic substitutes made of aluminum oxide (India™ stones) or silicon carbide (Crystolon™) are less expensive and just as effective as natural stones, though they tend to wear more quickly. An economical compromise is the use of an India™ stone for rough sharpening and whetting, and a hard Arkansas stone for honing and polishing. When using oilstones, wipe them often with a rag to prevent glazing. Do not use a heavy oil, as it inhibits the abrading process; a light machine oil cut with kerosene works best.

Waterstones are Japanese in origin, and cut much faster than oilstones. Because they use water, rather than oil as the lubricant, there is no oily mess left on clothes and workpieces. Waterstones come in finer grades than oilstones, making them popular with woodworkers who like to hone and polish. Because they are softer than oilstones, new abrasive is constantly exposed during use, and the slurry formed by the water will form a fine polishing paste.

Waterstones have their drawbacks, however. Because they are softer than oilstones, they must be trued more often (page 19).

Tools should be dried and wiped with oil thoroughly after sharpening to prevent rust. Waterstones also should be stored in water. If your shop is prone to cold temperatures, keep your waterstones from freezing, as they will shatter.

A COLLECTION OF BENCHSTONES

OILSTONES

Hard Black Arkansas
An extra-fine, 1000-grit natural stone used for razor-sharp honing of surgical, dental and other precision tools

Soft Arkansas
A medium, 500-grit natural stone used for initial sharpening of dull edges

Hard Arkansas
A fine, 800-grit natural stone used for honing tools to a sharp edge

Washita
A coarse, fast-cutting 350-grit natural stone used for flattening and lapping badly nicked tools

Combination stone
Also known as an India™ stone. A synthetic stone made from aluminum oxide with 90 grit on one face and 600 on the other; used for general sharpening and honing.

TRUING A BENCHSTONE

Lapping compound

Slurry

Lapping table

Flattening the stone

All benchstones will develop a hollow in the center after prolonged use. To true a benchstone, flatten it on a machined surface, such as glass pane or a lapping table. For oilstones, rub the surface with a circular motion *(left)* in a slurry made from a coarse lapping compound mixed with honing oil. Start with a coarse grit and work through finer grits until the stone is flat. To true a waterstone, use water instead of honing oil for the slurry, or wet/dry silicon carbide paper taped to the lapping surface.

WATERSTONES

Japanese finishing stone
An extra-fine, 1200-grit synthetic stone made from cerium oxide; used for final honing and polishing; small Nagura stone used to create slurry

Japanese coarse stone
A coarse, 180-grit synthetic stone made from silicone carbide; used for flattening and lapping badly nicked tools

Diamond stone
A hard synthetic stone made from microscopic diamond crystals bonded to solid steel plate; features a true, flat surface that will not wear like other stones. Available in a range of grits between 220 and 1200 for any sharpening or honing task

OTHER STONES

Slipstone
A shaped stone used for turning and carving tools, featuring both rounded and angled edges; a range of grits is available in both oil and water types

Gouge slipstone
A conical stone used for gouges; concave surface sharpens outside edge of tool, while convex surface deburrs the inside edge. A range of grits is available in both oil and water types

Ceramic stone
A fine, hard 1000-grit synthetic stone made from bonded aluminum oxide; used for honing. Needs no lubricant

BENCH GRINDERS

From squaring and sharpening plane irons to polishing chisels and turning tools, the bench grinder is a worthwhile addition to a woodworking shop's sharpening station.

Bench grinders are classified according to their wheel diameter. Standard 5- to 8-inch benchtop models, with ¼- to ¾-horsepower motors, are the most popular sizes. Larger wheels are better, as smaller wheels can produce exaggerated hollow-ground bevels. Grinders can be mounted on a work surface or fastened to a separate stand.

Rotating around 3500 rpm, a bench grinder removes steel faster than a sharpening stone. Unfortunately, it also heats up the tool, and you may lose the tool's temper. If the steel begins to change color during grinding, deepening to a true blue, the temper has been lost, and the tool must be reground. Motorized whetstones and wet/dry grinders feature water-bathed wheels that turn at slower speeds, such as 500 rpm, allowing you to grind tools without constantly dipping them in water for cooling.

Most grinders can be equipped with optional rubber sharpening wheels, cloth buffing wheels, and leather strop wheels in addition to standard abrasive wheels, which come in a variety of grits *(see below)*. Grinding wheels will eventually become dull and clogged with metal particles, and their edges may go out of square. A wheel dresser *(page 22)* can be used to true the face of a glazed wheel and square its edges.

The cutting edge of a skew chisel gets a sharpening on a wet/dry grinder. Because the large wheel of this type of grinder rotates relatively slowly and is continually bathed in water, the blade being sharpened remains cool, which reduces the risk of destroying its temper. Standard bench grinder wheels often rotate at speeds that are too fast for honing many tools; as a result, the tool's steel can easily overheat.

IDENTIFYING GRINDER WHEELS

STANDARD MARKING SYSTEM CHART			
ABRASIVE TYPE	**A**: Aluminum oxide	**C**: Silicon carbide	**Z**: Aluminum zirconium
ABRASIVE (GRAIN) SIZE	**Coarse:** 8, 10, 12, 14, 16, 20, 24 **Medium:** 30, 36, 46, 54, 60 **Fine:** 70, 80, 90, 100, 120, 150, 180		**Very fine:** 220, 240, 280, 320, 400, 500, 600
GRADE SCALE	Soft Medium Hard A B C D E F G H I J K L M N O P Q R S T U V W X Y Z		
STRUCTURE	Dense ————————————▶ Open 1 2 3 4 5 6 7 8 9 10 11 12 13 14 15 16 etc		
BOND TYPE	**B**: Resinoid **BF**: Resinoid reinforced **E**: Shellac **O**: Oxychloride **R**: Rubber **RF**: Rubber reinforced **S**: Silicate **V**: Vitrified		

Courtesy of the American National Standards Institute

Choosing a grinder wheel

The wheels supplied on grinders are usually too coarse for use with finer tools. A wide variety of replacement stones are available, but selecting the right one is no simple matter. You need to decipher the codes marked on the sides of the wheels, describing their composition and abrasive quality. The chart above will help you interpret these codes. (They are usually found sandwiched between two numerical manufacturer's symbols printed on the side of the stone.) If you plan to use a wheel to grind carbon-steel tools, and then hone with a benchstone, buy a wheel marked A 80 H 8V. This means the wheel is aluminum oxide (A), fine-grained (80), and relatively soft (H), with a medium structure or concentration of abrasives (8). The particles are bonded together by a process of heat and fusion known as vitrification (V). For high-speed steel tools, a medium hardness of I or J is better. If you plan to use your tools right off the grinder, choose a wheel with a grain size of 100 or 120.

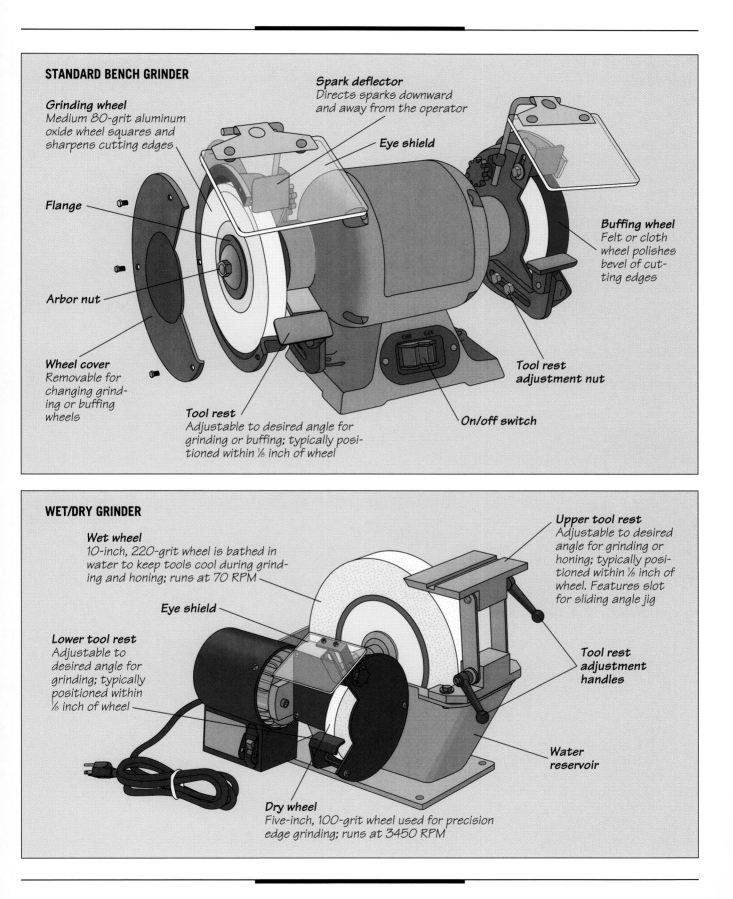

STANDARD BENCH GRINDER

Grinding wheel
Medium 80-grit aluminum oxide wheel squares and sharpens cutting edges

Spark deflector
Directs sparks downward and away from the operator

Eye shield

Buffing wheel
Felt or cloth wheel polishes bevel of cutting edges

Flange

Arbor nut

Wheel cover
Removable for changing grinding or buffing wheels

Tool rest
Adjustable to desired angle for grinding or buffing; typically positioned within ⅛ inch of wheel

Tool rest adjustment nut

On/off switch

WET/DRY GRINDER

Wet wheel
10-inch, 220-grit wheel is bathed in water to keep tools cool during grinding and honing; runs at 70 RPM

Upper tool rest
Adjustable to desired angle for grinding or honing; typically positioned within ⅛ inch of wheel. Features slot for sliding angle jig

Eye shield

Lower tool rest
Adjustable to desired angle for grinding; typically positioned within ⅛ inch of wheel

Tool rest adjustment handles

Water reservoir

Dry wheel
Five-inch, 100-grit wheel used for precision edge grinding; runs at 3450 RPM

DRESSING A GRINDING WHEEL

Truing the wheel

A grinding wheel should be trued when ridges or hollows appear on the stone or if it becomes discolored. You can use either a star-wheel or diamond-point dresser. To use a star-wheel dresser *(right)*, move the grinder's tool rest away from the wheel. With the guard in position, switch on the grinder and butt the tip of the dresser against the wheel. Then, with your index finger resting against the tool rest, move the dresser from side to side. To use a diamond-point dresser *(below)*, hold the device between the index finger and the thumb of one hand, set it on the tool rest, and advance it toward the wheel until your index finger contacts the tool rest. Move either dresser back and forth across the wheel until the edges are square and you have exposed fresh abrasive.

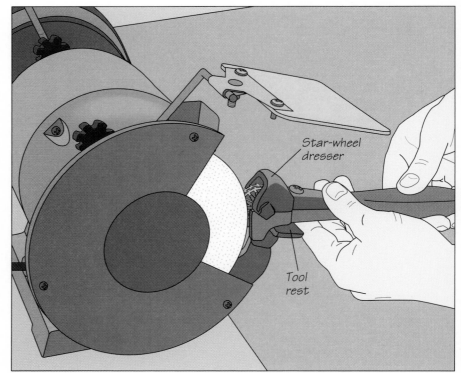

Star-wheel dresser

Tool rest

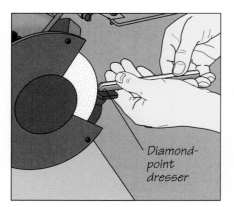

Diamond-point dresser

SHOP TIP

Reversing wheel guards for buffing

Because they spin in the same direction as the standard grinding wheel mounted on the left-hand side of a bench grinder, neoprene or felt buffing wheels mounted on the right-hand require a change of tool position for buffing so the tool does not catch in the wheel. Another solution is to reverse the right-hand wheel guard to expose the rear of the wheel *(right)*. In this position, the buffing wheel spins away from you instead of towards you, so you can buff the tool at the same angle as you do when grinding it.

BUILD IT YOURSELF

A MOBILE SHARPENING DOLLY

A sharpening station is more than just a dedicated space for sharpening. It is a way of keeping all of your benchstones, grinding jigs, and sharpening accessories clean and well-organized. The sharpening station shown below is essentially a sturdy low bench with a storage shelf. The unit is built from ¾-inch plywood and 1-by-3 stock. By adding locking casters, it becomes a mobile sharpening dolly that you can wheel about the shop to wherever you need to sharpen: at the lathe, the carving bench, or near the sink.

To build the dolly, cut the base from ¾-inch plywood. Make it large enough to incorporate all your sharpening gear so that it is not too cluttered; up to 3-by-6 feet is a good size. Screw four corner blocks to the underside of the base, and fasten a locking caster on each block.

To strengthen the dolly, cut the pieces for the skirts and legs from 1-by-3 stock. The legs should be long enough for the top to sit at a

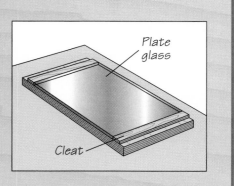

comfortable height; between 32 and 36 inches is right for most people. Screw the leg pieces together, then attach the skirts to the legs' inside faces. Fasten the shelf and the top to the skirts. If desired, glue a water- and oil-proof plastic laminate work surface to the top.

Once you have built the dolly, mount a standard bench grinder or wet/dry grinder to the end of the bench so that both wheels are accessible. Secure a lapping table *(inset)* at the opposite end for lapping and flattening stones. This is simply a piece of ⅜-inch tempered plate glass secured with cleats to a piece of ½-inch plywood, fastened to the top. Have the glass cut three times larger than your largest bench stone.

Now mount your most commonly used benchstones either by using cleats or screwing their wooden storage boxes to the tabletop; countersink the fasteners. Other accessories could include a vise or a portable light positioned to shine on the grinder.

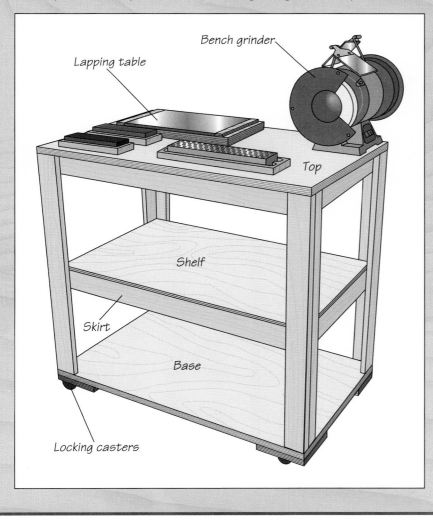

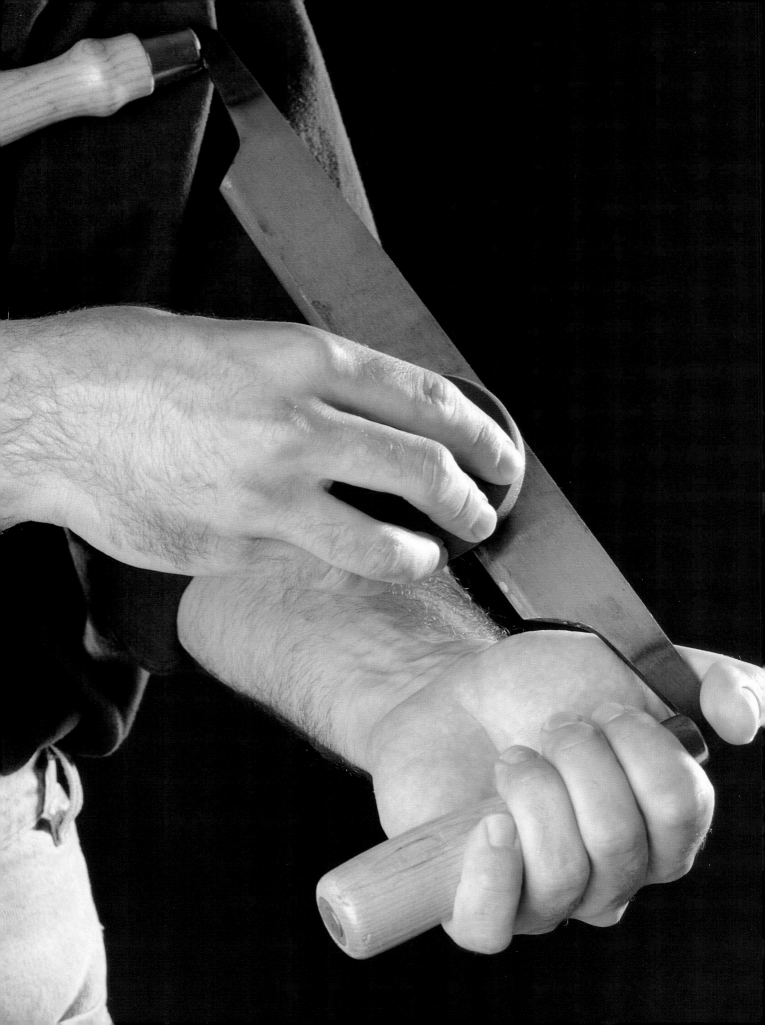

SHARPENING AND MAINTAINING HAND TOOLS

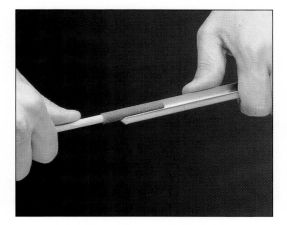

The simple shop-made jig shown above, consisting of a dowel wrapped in a piece of emery cloth, is ideal for cleaning and removing burrs from the rounded edge of gouges.

Despite the proliferation of power tools in recent years, hand tools are still an important part of the modern woodworking shop. Handsaws, chisels, and planes play a vital role in many cabinetmaking tasks, from cutting joints and chopping mortises to smoothing stock. For some crafts, like carving and turning, hand-cutting tools such as gouges and skew chisels are virtually indispensable.

One distinct advantage that hand tools offer over their electrically powered counterparts is that they are relatively straightforward to sharpen and maintain. With hand tools, there are no hidden circuit boards or sealed components, no carbide-tipped blades that must be sharpened professionally. With most hand tools, such as saws and chisels, what you see is what you get: a handle, often made of wood, and a steel cutting edge. True, not all hand tools are quite this simple. Bench planes feature screws and levers for adjusting the angle and position of the cutting edge. Still, all the parts are easily accessible, allowing you to sharpen and maintain the tool in the shop. In fact, with a little elbow grease and the right materials, you can even restore a rusty old hand plane to better condition than when it was first bought *(page 40)*.

Setting yourself up for hand tool sharpening and maintenance requires no great investment. All you need are solvents for cleaning, a few commercial devices for adjusting blades, stones and files for honing and sharpening—and the proper technique. The following pages will show you how to care for and sharpen the most commonly used hand tools, from handsaws *(page 26)* and chisels and gouges *(page 30)* to bench planes *(page 39)*, scrapers *(page 46)*, and bits for braces and hand drills *(page 55)*.

The work is relatively easy, but the rewards are considerable. Hand tools that are well sharpened and properly maintained will improve the quality of your projects and prolong the life of your tools.

The cutting edge of a drawknife is honed by an axe-stone. Holding one handle of the tool as shown at left and butting the other handle against the crook of the arm exposes the entire edge for sharpening.

HANDSAWS

S harpening a handsaw is a three-step operation. As shown on page 28, the process begins with jointing, or filing the tips of the teeth so that they are all the same height. This is followed by setting the teeth to the correct angle. This ensures that the blade cuts straight and does not stick in the kerf. Setting involves bending the teeth alternately to each side of the blade's centerline. The final step in the process is sharpening itself, typically with a file.

Not all handsaws are identical. The shape, spacing, and set of the teeth vary according to the type of cutting the saw will perform. The spacing between teeth is usually expressed in TPI, or teeth per inch. The following pages describe how to sharpen rip saws, combination saws, and both Japanese and Western-style crosscut saws. Because of their very fine teeth, dovetail and tenon saws should be sent out to a professional for sharpening.

A commercial saw set bends the teeth of a combination saw to the proper angle with the blade clamped in a bench vise. Setting the teeth of a saw blade is a key step in the sharpening procees, producing a kerf that prevents the blade from binding.

ANATOMY OF SAW BLADES AND FILING ANGLES

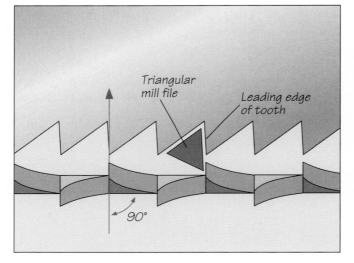

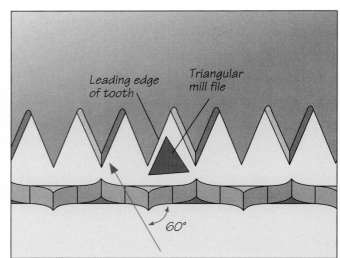

Filing ripsaw teeth

Ripsaws have widely spaced teeth with from five to seven teeth per inch (TPI). They also have a more pronounced set than other saws. Both features enable them to cut quickly along the grain. As shown above, the leading edges of rip teeth are almost vertical. To sharpen the teeth, use a triangular mill file, drawing it straight across each tooth at a 90° angle to the blade axis.

Filing combination teeth

Combination saws are dual-purpose saws that can be used for both rip cuts and crosscuts, although they rip more slowly than a rip saw and cut more roughly than a crosscut saw. Combination teeth slope forward and backward at the same angle (about 60°) and both edges are beveled. Sharpen both edges using a triangular mill file *(above)*, tilting the handle of the file down slightly.

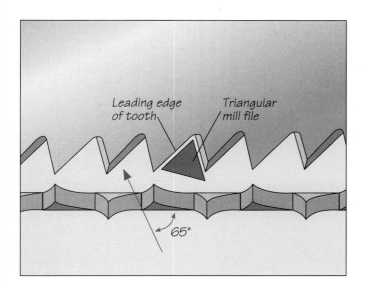

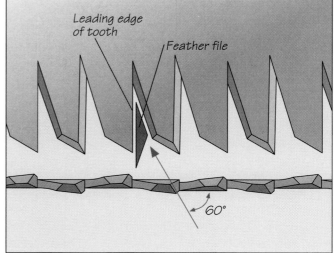

Sharpening crosscut teeth

The teeth of a crosscut saw are closely spaced—eight to 12 TPI is typical—and they have very little set. Crosscut teeth feature sloped leading edges with bevels, which enable them to cut cleanly across the grain. As with rip saws, the teeth are sharpened with a triangular mill file. Hold the file at the same angle as the bevel, which is typically 65° *(above)*.

Sharpening Japanese crosscut teeth

Japanese saws, which cut on the pull stroke, have tall, narrow teeth with very little set. Also, the teeth are beveled on leading and trailing edges, and on the tips. All edges should be sharpened with a feather file held at about a 60° angle to the blade *(above)*.

SHOP TIP

A saw holder

Storing handsaws properly will both eliminate clutter and keep the tools accessible and safe from damage. The simple device shown here can be used to hang a saw on the shop wall in plain view. Cut a wood scrap a little thicker than the saw handle to the same profile as the opening in the handle; use the opening as a template. Fasten the piece to the wall at a convenient height, then screw a small block with rounded ends to the piece as a turnbuckle. Make the turnbuckle shorter than the width of the handle opening, but longer than the height. Leave the screw slightly loose so that you can pivot the turnbuckle vertically to secure the saw to the wall.

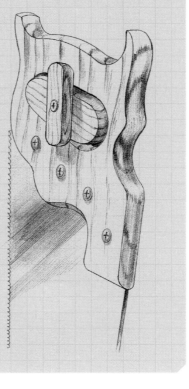

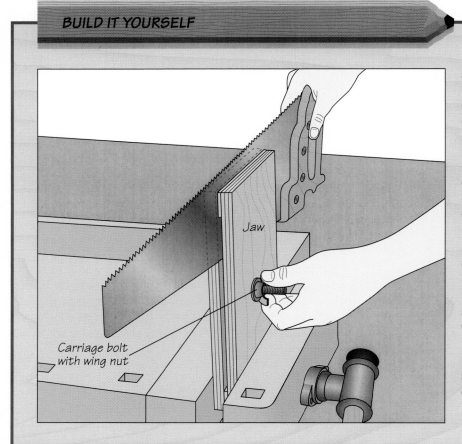

BUILD IT YOURSELF

Jaw

Carriage bolt
with wing nut

A BENCH VISE SAW HOLDER
Secured in a vise, the simple jig shown at left will hold a saw at a convenient height for sharpening. Make the jaws from two pieces of ½-inch plywood about 10 inches long and 7 inches wide. Then saw two ⅛-inch-thick strips and glue them along the inside faces of the jaws, flush with the top end; the strips will grip the saw blade. Fasten the two jaws together near the bottom end, screwing a strip of ¼-inch plywood between them. Finally, bore a hole for a carriage bolt through the middle of the jaws and install the bolt with a washer and wing nut.

To use the jig, secure the bottom end in your vise. Loosen the wing nut, slip a saw blade between the jaws, and tighten the nut to hold the saw securely.

SHARPENING A HANDSAW

1 Jointing the teeth
Mount the saw teeth-up in a vise with a wood pad on each side of the blade for protection. Install a flat mill bastard file in a commercial saw jointing jig. Hold the jig flat against the side of the blade and pass the file back and forth across the full length of the teeth *(right)*. This will flatten all of the teeth to the same height. A few passes should be sufficient.

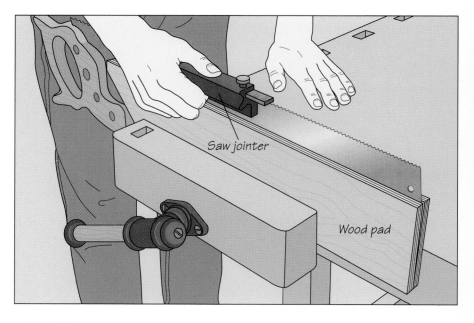

Saw jointer

Wood pad

2 Setting the teeth

With the saw still in the vise, adjust a saw set to the same TPI as the blade. Starting at either end of the blade, position the first tooth that is bent away from you between the anvil and the punch block. Squeeze the handle to set the tooth *(right)*. Work your way down the length of the blade, setting all teeth that are bent away from you. Then turn the saw around in the vise and repeat the process on the remaining teeth.

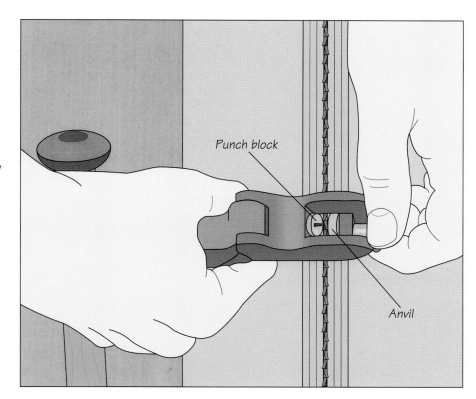

Punch block

Anvil

File stroke direction

3 Filing the teeth.

Refer to the appropriate illustration on page 26 or 27 for the proper file and filing angle for the saw you are sharpening. For the crosscut saw shown at left, hold a triangular file at about a 65° angle to the blade with its handle tilted down slightly. As you file the teeth, work from one end of the blade to the other, filing all the teeth that are set in one direction. Then turn the saw around to sharpen the remaining teeth.

CHISELS AND GOUGES

Chisels and gouges must have razor-sharp edges to work properly. Sharpening a standard woodworking chisel is simple; all you need is a combination sharpening stone. For most chisels and gouges, you will have to hone and polish the cutting edge as well as produce the correct bevel angle for the blade.

Well-sharpened blades are essential for turning chisels and gouges. Dull cutting edges not only produce poor results; they are also more difficult to control and dangerous to use. This section of the chapter explains how to sharpen and refurbish a wide range of chisels and gouges.

Even the most rusted and pitted blade can be renewed with steel wool, mineral spirits, clean rags, and a bit of elbow grease.

INVENTORY OF CHISELS AND GOUGES

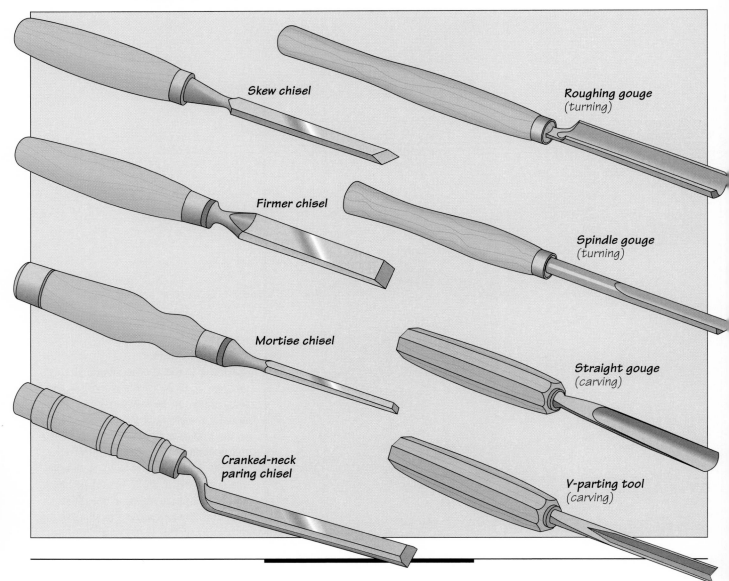

Skew chisel

Firmer chisel

Mortise chisel

Cranked-neck
paring chisel

Roughing gouge
(turning)

Spindle gouge
(turning)

Straight gouge
(carving)

V-parting tool
(carving)

REPLACING A CHISEL OR GOUGE HANDLE

1 Turning the new handle
Turn a new handle for a chisel or gouge on the lathe. Cut a blank from a dense, strong hardwood like ash or hickory. The grain should run the length of the blank. A piece that is 1½ to 2 inches square and a few inches longer than the finished length you need will yield a suitable handle. Mount the piece between centers on the lathe and turn it to a smooth cylinder using a roughing gouge. Buy a brass ferrule for the handle. Then use a parting tool to turn a tenon on one end of the blank to accommodate the ferrule. Measure the inside diameter of the ferrule with dial calipers *(right)* and size the tenon to fit tightly.

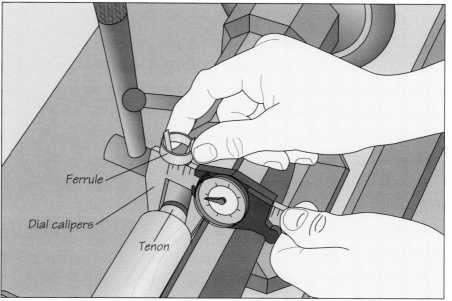

Ferrule

Dial calipers

Tenon

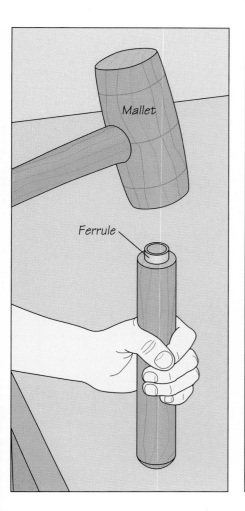

Mallet

Ferrule

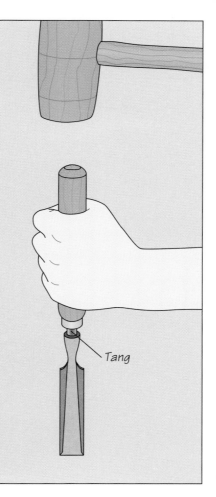

Tang

2 Mounting the ferrule and the blade
Remove the handle from the lathe, set it end-down on a work surface, and tap the ferrule in place with a mallet *(far left)*. Next, remount the handle on the lathe and shape it with a skew chisel and spindle gouge. Once you are satisfied with the handle's shape and feel, bore a hole in the tenon end to accommodate the tang of the blade. Bore the hole on the lathe with a Jacobs chuck attached to the tailstock; make sure the hole is centered in the blank. The hole's diameter and depth depend on the type of tang. For a round-section, untapered tang, the hole should be 2 to 3 inches deep and equal to the tang diameter. For a square-section, tapered tang, drill two holes as you would counterbore for a screw and plug: Make the top half the same diameter as the tang 1¼ inches from the tip and the bottom half the same width as the tang ¾ inch from its tip. Insert the blade into the handle and rap the butt end of the handle with a mallet *(near left)*.

SHARPENING A STANDARD CHISEL

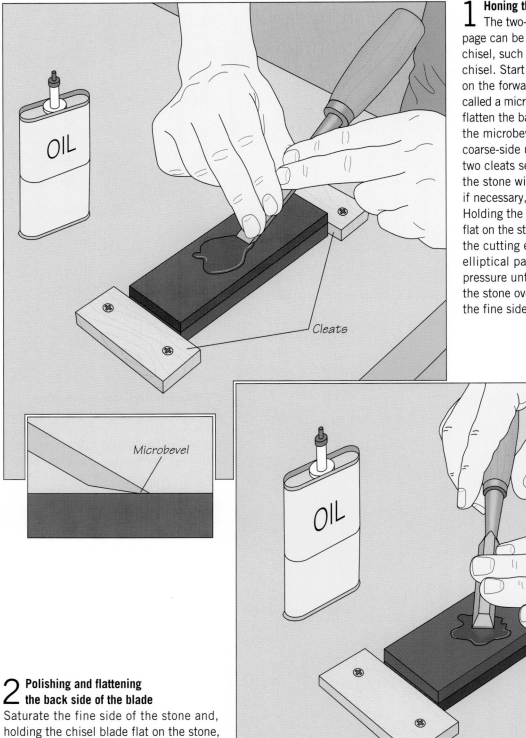

1 Honing the cutting edge
The two-step procedure shown on this page can be used to sharpen any standard chisel, such as a firmer, paring, or mortise chisel. Start by honing a secondary bevel on the forward edge of the existing one—called a microbevel *(inset)*—then polish and flatten the back side of the blade. To form the microbevel, lay a combination stone coarse-side up on a work surface between two cleats secured with screws. Saturate the stone with the appropriate lubricant, if necessary, until it pools on the surface. Holding the blade with the existing bevel flat on the stone, raise it about 5° and slide the cutting edge along the stone in long, elliptical passes *(left)*. Apply moderate pressure until a microbevel forms. Turn the stone over and make a few passes on the fine side.

Cleats

Microbevel

2 Polishing and flattening the back side of the blade
Saturate the fine side of the stone and, holding the chisel blade flat on the stone, bevel-side up, move it in a circular pattern *(right)* until the flat side of the cutting edge is smooth.

SHARPENING A ROUGHING-OUT GOUGE

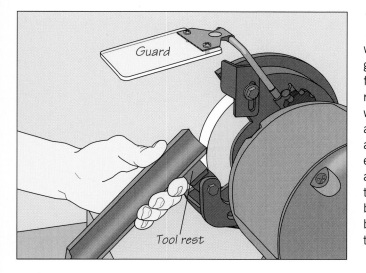

Guard

Tool rest

1 Grinding the cutting edge
Sharpen a roughing-out gouge on a bench grinder equipped with a medium grinding wheel and a felt wheel. Position the guard and turn on the machine. Holding the blade between the fingers and thumb of one hand, set the cutting edge on the tool rest and advance it until the bevel lightly contacts the grinding wheel. If you want to change the bevel angle of the cutting edge, adjust the tool rest to the desired angle. With your index finger against the tool rest, roll the blade on the wheel *(left)* until the entire edge is ground. Keep the bevel flat against the wheel at all times. Continue, checking the blade regularly, until the cutting edge is sharp and the bevel angle is correct. To prevent the blade from overheating, occasionally dip it in water if it is carbon steel, or remove it from the wheel if it is high-speed steel to let it cool down.

BUILD IT YOURSELF

GOUGE-SHARPENING JIG

The jig shown at right will hold a gouge so that the blade contacts the grinding wheel at the correct angle. The dimensions in the illustration will accommodate most turning gouges. Cut the base and guide from ½-inch plywood. Screw the guide together and fasten it to the base with countersunk screws from underneath. Make the guide opening large enough for the arm to slide through freely.

Cut the arm from 1-by-2 stock and the tool support from ½-inch plywood. Screw the two parts of the tool support together, then fasten the bottom to the arm flush with one end. For the V-block, cut a small block to size and saw a 90° wedge out of one side. Glue the piece to the tool support.

To use the jig, secure it to a work surface so the arm lines up directly under the grinding wheel. Seat the gouge handle in the V-block and slide the arm so the beveled edge of the gouge sits flat on the grinding wheel. Clamp the arm in place. Then, with the gouge clear of the wheel, switch on the grinder and reposition the tool on the jig. Roll the beveled edge across the wheel *(right, bottom)*.

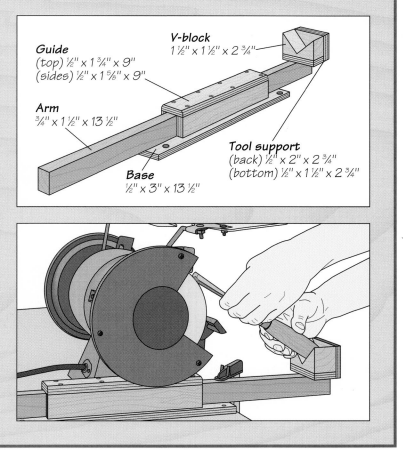

Guide
(top) ½" x 1 ¾" x 9"
(sides) ½" x 1 ⅝" x 9"

V-block
1 ½" x 1 ½" x 2 ¾"

Arm
¾" x 1 ½" x 13 ½"

Base
½" x 3" x 13 ½"

Tool support
(back) ½" x 2" x 2 ¾"
(bottom) ½" x 1 ½" x 2 ¾"

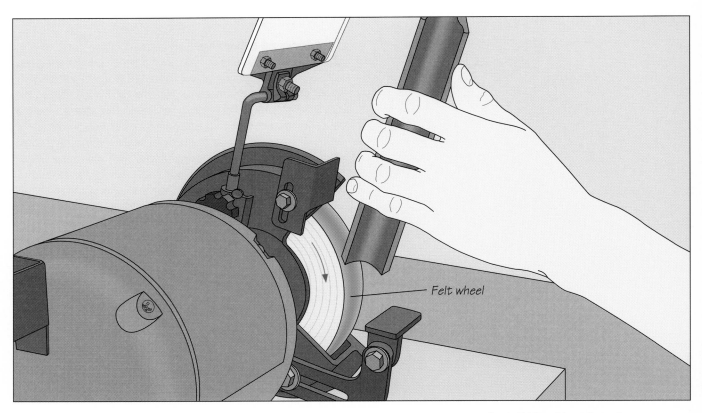

Felt wheel

SHOP TIP

Shop-made honing guides and rust removers
The inside edges of gouges can be difficult to hone and strop if you do not have a slipstone or strop with the correct shape. You can make a gouge-honing guide by wrapping a dowel with 600-grit sandpaper (near right). For stropping, simply fold a strip of leather to fit the inside edge of the gouge (far right). You can also use these jigs to clean rust or pitting from an old blade.

2 **Polishing the cutting edge**
Shift to the grinder's felt wheel and move the tool rest out of the way. Hold a stick of polishing compound against the felt wheel to impregnate it with abrasive. Grip the handle of the gouge in your right hand and hold the blade between the fingers and thumbs of your left hand. Then, with the gouge almost vertical, set the bevel flat against the wheel. Lightly roll the blade from side to side against the wheel to polish the bevel. A slight burr will form on the inside edge of the tool. To feel for the burr, run your finger gently across the inside edge of the blade. To remove it, roll the inside face of the blade against the wheel until the burr rubs off. Avoid overbuffing the blade; this will dull the cutting edge. Test the tool for sharpness by cutting a scrap across the grain. The blade should produce a clean shaving.

A SPINDLE GOUGE

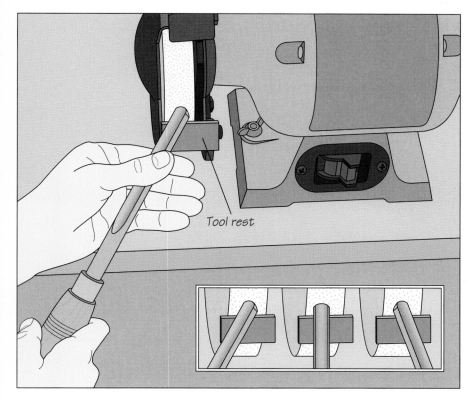

Tool rest

1 Sharpening on a bench grinder
Position the guard properly and turn on the grinder. Holding the blade between the fingers and thumb of one hand, set the blade flat on the tool rest and advance it until the blade lightly touches the stone *(left)*. Adjust the tool rest to create the desired bevel angle. Roll the cutting edge on the wheel and pivot the handle from left to right while keeping the bevel flat on the grinding wheel at all times *(inset)*. Continue rolling the blade and moving the tool handle from side to side until the edge is sharpened, stopping frequently to check the grind and cool the tip. Hone the cutting edge and remove the burr by hand, as shown below, or use the grinder's felt wheel *(page 34)*.

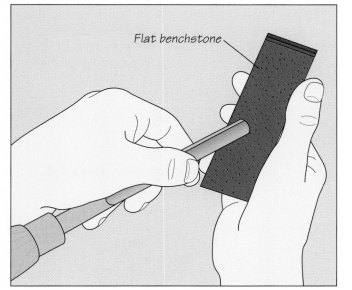

Flat benchstone

2 Honing the cutting edge
Once the bevel has been sharpened on the grinder, use a flat benchstone to polish the tool to a razor-sharp edge. Saturate the stone with oil, then roll the outside bevel across the abrasive surface *(above)* to hone the bevel on the cutting edge.

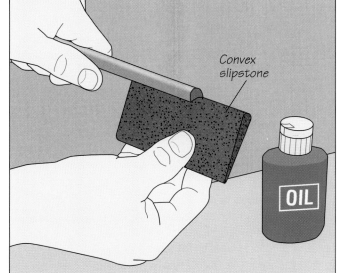

Convex slipstone

OIL

3 Removing the burr
Use a convex slipstone matching the curvature of the gouge to remove the burr that forms on the inside of the cutting edge. Lubricate the slipstone if needed and hone the inside edge until the burr is eliminated.

SHARPENING A CARVING GOUGE

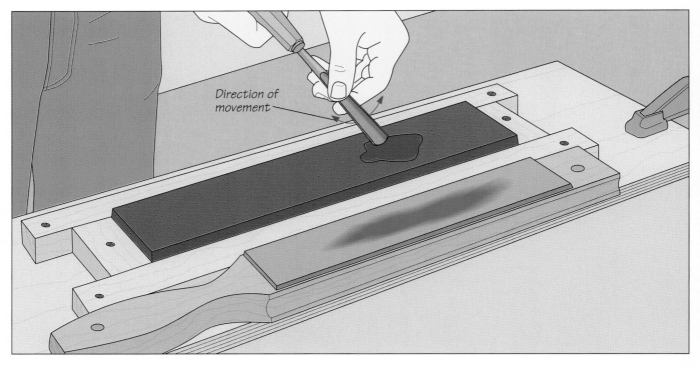

Direction of
movement

1 Whetting the outside bevel

Set an oilstone on a plywood base, screw cleats to the base around the stone to keep it from moving, and clamp the base to a work surface. (The leather strop is used to polish the outside bevel in step 4). Saturate the stone, then set the outside bevel of the gouge flat on it. Starting at one end, move the blade back and forth along the stone with a rhythmic motion, simultaneously rolling the tool so the entire bevel contacts the sharp-

ening surface *(above)*. Avoid rocking the blade too far, as this will tend to round over its corners and blunt the cutting edge. Continue until the bevel is smooth and a burr forms on the inside edge of the blade. You can also carry out this step on a grinder, as shown on page 33, but if you use the machine be sure to adjust the angle of the tool rest to match the bevel angle of the gouge.

2 Honing an inside bevel

Once you have sharpened the gouge's outside bevel, use a conical slipstone to hone a slight inside bevel on the blade and to remove the burr formed in step 1. Put a few drops of oil on the cutting edge of the gouge. Then, holding the stone on a work surface, move the blade back and forth along the stone making sure that you keep the cutting edge well away from your fingers. Continue until the burr is removed and an inside bevel of approximately 5° forms.

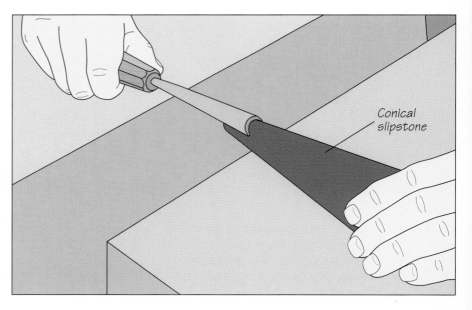

Conical
slipstone

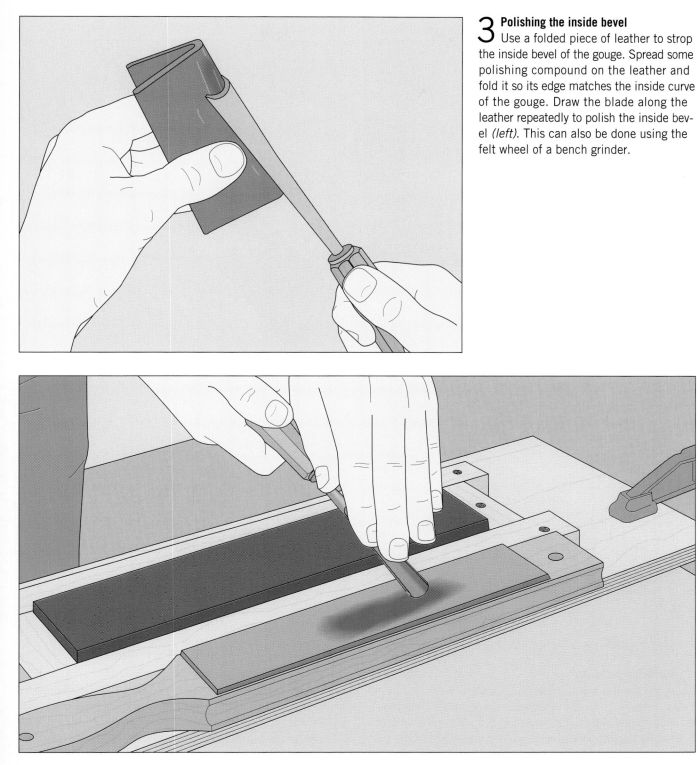

3 Polishing the inside bevel

Use a folded piece of leather to strop the inside bevel of the gouge. Spread some polishing compound on the leather and fold it so its edge matches the inside curve of the gouge. Draw the blade along the leather repeatedly to polish the inside bevel *(left)*. This can also be done using the felt wheel of a bench grinder.

4 Polishing the outside bevel

Spread some polishing compound on the strop and use the same rolling technique shown in step 1 to polish the outside bevel *(above)*. Check the inside bevel; if a burr has formed, repeat step 3. You can also use a bench grinder and a felt wheel impregnated with polishing compound *(page 34)* for this task.

SHARPENING A V-TOOL

1 Whetting the outside edges
Sharpen each side of a V-tool separately. Set up and saturate an oilstone as you would to sharpen a carving gouge *(page 36)*. Hone one outside bevel of the V-tool as you would a chisel *(page 32)*, moving the blade back and forth along the length of the stone and keeping the bevel flat on the stone. Repeat on the other side of the V *(right)*. Stop working when you have removed the rough marks from the ground edge and a small burr forms on the inside of the edge.

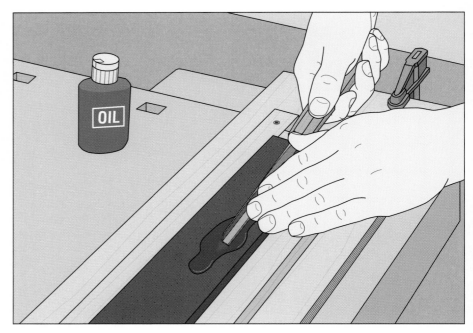

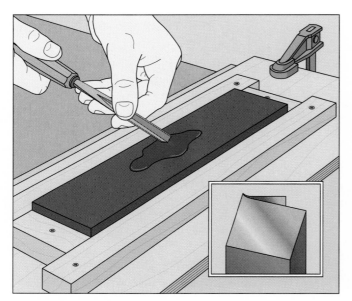

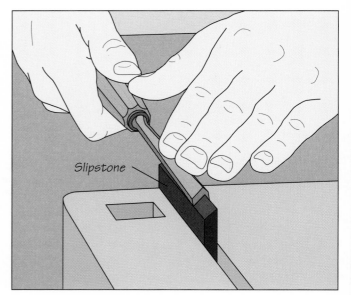

Slipstone

2 Removing the hook
When you sharpen the outside bevels of a V-tool, a hook of excess metal will form at the apex of the V *(inset)*. This hook must be ground away before you hone the inside bevel in step 3. Holding the tool on the stone, roll the corner across the surface *(above)*. Move the tool from end to end along the stone until you wear away the hook and an outside bevel forms at the apex of the V, forming one continuous beveled edge. This process will create a burr in the center of the inside edge, which is removed in step 3.

3 Honing the inside bevel
To remove the burr formed in steps 1 and 2, and hone an inside bevel, use a triangular slipstone that matches the angle of the V-tool blade as closely as possible. Clamp the stone securely in a bench vise and saturate it with oil. To avoid crushing the stone, do not overtighten the vise. Draw the end of the blade's inside edge back and forth along the stone *(above)*, applying light downward pressure until the burr is removed and a slight inside bevel forms. To finish, polish the edge with a leather strop *(page 37)* or the felt wheel of a grinder *(page 34)*.

BENCH PLANES

A good-quality bench plane can be costly, but there is no reason why it should not last a lifetime—or two. This section shows how to care for a plane, and includes information on sharpening and adjusting the tool. You can save yourself some money—without sacrificing a whit of quality—by refurbishing an old plane *(page 40)*. Even a tool that has been abused and discarded by someone else can be brought back to life.

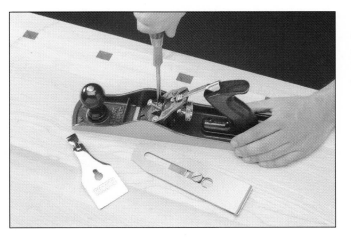

Tightening the frog setscrews is a fundamental step in the reassembly of the bench plane (page 45).

ANATOMY OF A BENCH PLANE

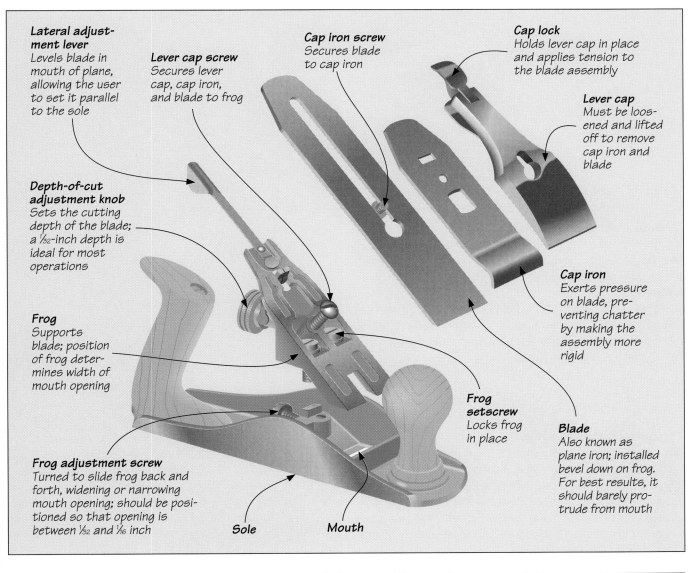

Lateral adjustment lever
Levels blade in mouth of plane, allowing the user to set it parallel to the sole

Depth-of-cut adjustment knob
Sets the cutting depth of the blade; a ¹⁄₃₂-inch depth is ideal for most operations

Frog
Supports blade; position of frog determines width of mouth opening

Frog adjustment screw
Turned to slide frog back and forth, widening or narrowing mouth opening; should be positioned so that opening is between ¹⁄₃₂ and ¹⁄₁₆ inch

Lever cap screw
Secures lever cap, cap iron, and blade to frog

Cap iron screw
Secures blade to cap iron

Cap lock
Holds lever cap in place and applies tension to the blade assembly

Lever cap
Must be loosened and lifted off to remove cap iron and blade

Cap iron
Exerts pressure on blade, preventing chatter by making the assembly more rigid

Frog setscrew
Locks frog in place

Blade
Also known as plane iron; installed bevel down on frog. For best results, it should barely protrude from mouth

Sole

Mouth

REFURBISHING A BENCH PLANE

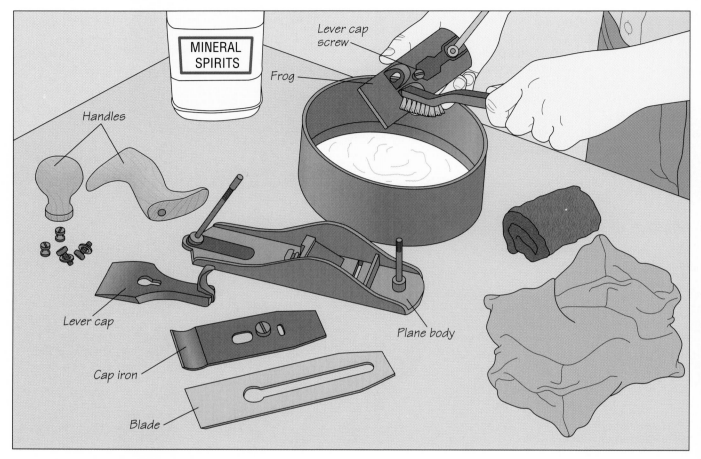

1 **Disassembling and cleaning the plane**
Refer to the anatomy illustration on page 39 to help you take the plane apart. Start by loosening the lever cap screw and releasing the cap lock, then take off the lever cap, cap iron, and blade and set them aside. Next, loosen and remove the frog setscrews and separate the frog from the sole of the plane. You can also unscrew the front and back handles from the body. Clean each part individually using a brass-bristled brush dipped in mineral spirits *(above)*.

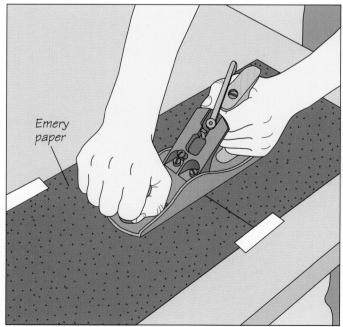

2 **Lapping the sole of the plane**
Tape a length of emery paper to a smooth and flat surface, such as a glass plate or saw table. Reattach the handles and the frog to the body of the plane, then slide the sole along the emery paper, applying even pressure to keep the sole flat *(right)*. Continue lapping the sole until the metal on its bottom surface is uniformly bright and clean, indicating that the sole is level. Check the sole for square *(step 3)* periodically.

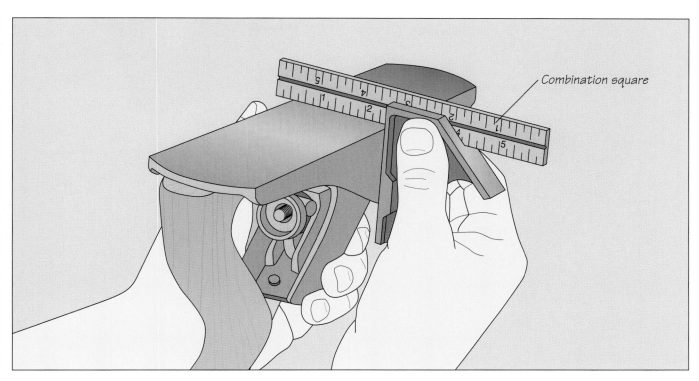

Combination square

3 Checking the sole for square

The bottom and sides of the plane's sole should be exactly at 90° to each other. Holding the plane in one hand, butt a combination square against the bottom and one side of the sole *(above)*. Repeat for the other side. The surfaces should be square both ways. If not, you will need to continue lapping the sole and the sides.

SHARPENING A PLANE BLADE

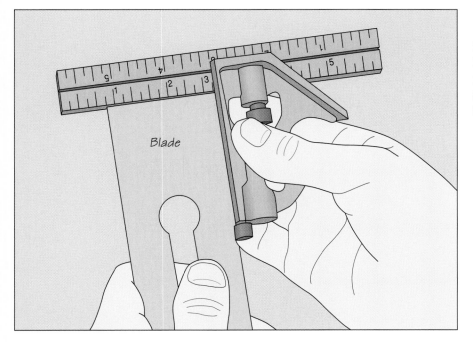

Blade

1 Checking the cutting edge for square

Use a combination square to determine whether the cutting edge of the plane blade is square to the sides *(left)*. If it is not, square the cutting edge on a bench grinder, making sure to adjust the grinder's tool rest at 90° to the wheel.

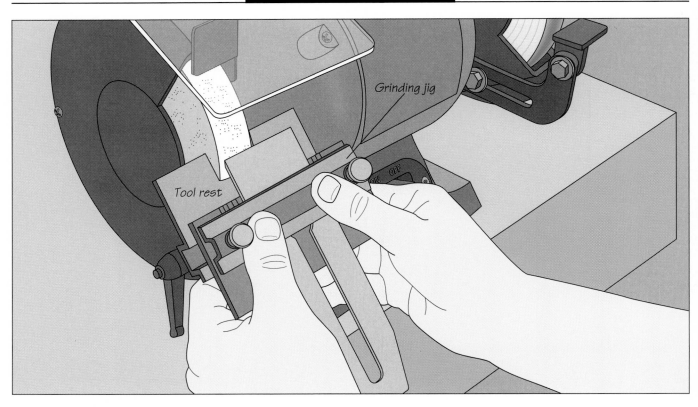

Grinding jig

Tool rest

2 Creating a hollow-ground bevel

Sharpening a plane blade involves three steps: creating a bevel on the blade's cutting edge, honing a microbevel on the first bevel, and removing the burr that results from the honing process. To create the first bevel, clamp the blade bevel-down in a commercial grinding jig and adjust the tool rest to create a 30° bevel. Holding the jig on the tool rest, advance it toward the wheel until the cutting edge makes contact *(above)*. Slide the blade side-to-side across the wheel, pressing lightly. Check the cutting edge periodically and stop grinding when the bevel forms.

SHOP TIP

Grinding with a sander
If you do not own a bench grinder, you can grind a plane blade on a belt sander. Install a 100-grit belt, mount the tool upside down in a stand, and secure the stand to a work surface. Turn on the sander and hold the beveled side of the blade on the belt at the appropriate angle.

3 Honing the microbevel

Once you sharpen the plane blade's cutting edge on a grinder, as in step 2, the result will be a hollow-ground bevel *(inset, left)*. If you did the job by hand on a sharpening stone, you will obtain a flat bevel *(inset, right)*. In either case, you need to hone a microbevel on the first bevel. Place a combination sharpening stone fine side up on a work surface. Screw cleats to the table against the stone to keep it from moving. For a hollow-ground bevel, clamp the blade in a commercial angle-setting honing guide with the bevel touching the stone. Saturate the stone with the appropriate lubricant and then, holding the honing guide, slide the blade back and forth from end to end along the sharpening surface *(right)*. Apply moderate pressure until a microbevel forms. If you are starting with a flat bevel, clamp the blade in a commercial angle-setting honing guide with the bevel touching the stone. Then raise the angle of the blade a few degrees and complete the operation as for a hollow-ground bevel.

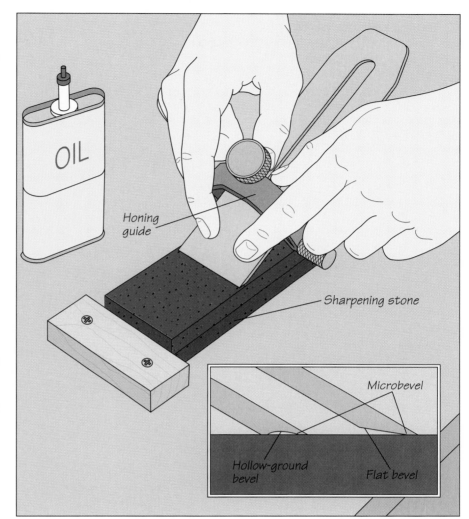

Honing guide

Sharpening stone

Microbevel

Hollow-ground bevel

Flat bevel

OIL

4 Lapping the burr

The honing process will create a thin ridge of metal, or burr, on the flat face of the blade. To remove the burr, saturate the fine side of the stone again. Holding the blade perfectly flat on the stone, bevel side up *(left)*, move it in a circular pattern until the flat side of the cutting edge is smooth.

5 **Testing the blade for sharpness**
Clamp a softwood board to a work surface and, holding the blade bevel-side up in your hands, cut across the grain of the surface *(right)*. A sharp blade will cleanly slice a sliver of wood from the board without tearing the wood fibers.

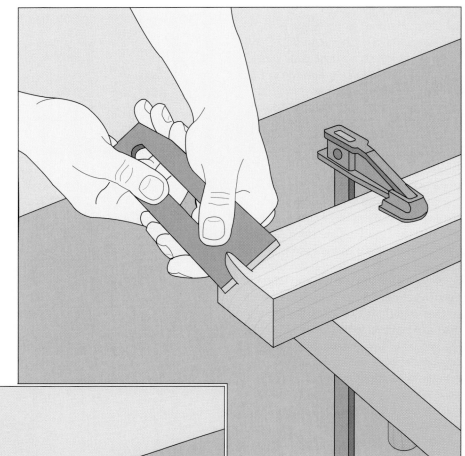

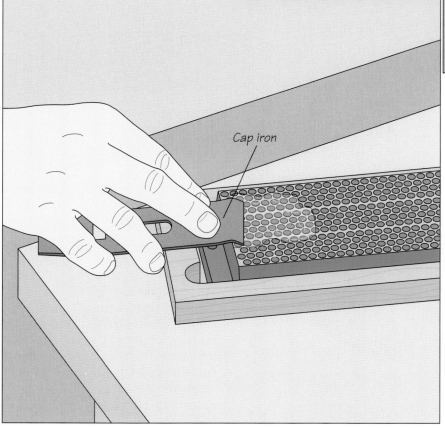

Cap iron

6 **Honing the end of the cap iron**
Secure a benchstone to your work surface; in the illustration at left, a diamond stone, which should be lubricated with water, is shown in its own box. Set the front portion of the cap iron that contacts the blade flat on the stone and slide it in a circular pattern on the surface *(left)*. Continue until the tip of the cap iron is perfectly flat. This will guarantee that wood chips will not become trapped between the iron and the blade once the two pieces are reassembled.

ASSEMBLING AND ADJUSTING A BENCH PLANE

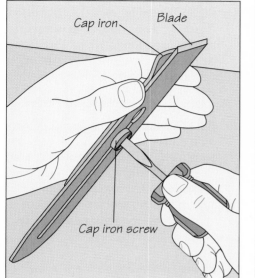

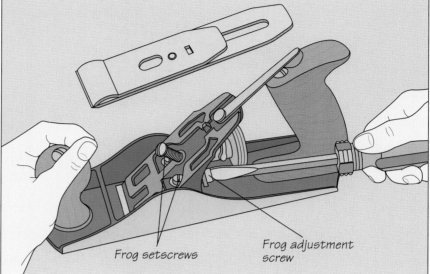

1 Positioning the blade assembly

Position the cap iron on the top face of the blade extending about 1⁄16 inch beyond the end of the cap iron. Tighten the cap iron screw *(above, left)*. Then place the blade assembly—including the blade, cap iron, and lever cap—in position on the frog. The gap between the front edge of the blade and the front of the mouth should be between 1⁄32 and 1⁄16 inch. If the gap is too wide or narrow, remove the blade assembly and loosen both frog setscrews about 1⁄4 turn. Then adjust the frog adjustment screw to set the proper gap *(above, right)*. Tighten the setscrews and reposition the blade assembly on the frog, securing it in place with the cap lock.

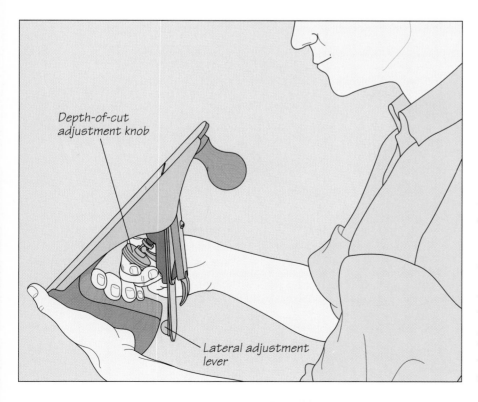

2 Centering the blade and adjusting the depth of cut

Holding the plane upside down, move the lateral adjustment lever until the cutting edge is parallel to the sole and centered in the mouth. To set the cutting depth, turn the depth-of-cut adjustment knob so the blade protrudes from the mouth *(left)*. About 1⁄32 inch is desirable; less for highly figured woods. Confirm the setting with a test cut on a scrap board. The shavings should be paper-thin.

SCRAPERS

P roperly honed, a hand or cabinet scraper is unsurpassed for smoothing and flattening a wood surface before finishing. For either type of scraper, sharpening is a four-step process, shown beginning on page 47. First, the edges of the scraper are filed square, then honed, and finally turned over into a burr and a hook *(page 48)*. You can produce the burr and the hook in two steps with a standard burnisher, like the one shown below, or create the hook in one operation with a variable burnisher *(photo, left)*. The result is a cutting edge that should be capable of slicing paper-thin curls of wood from a workpiece.

Honing a hand scraper is simple work with the help of the variable burnisher shown at left. The device features a carbide rod mounted within the wood body. A knob on the top adjusts the angle of the rod, providing precise control of the burnishing angle, while the jig is run back and forth over the cutting edge.

INVENTORY OF SCRAPERS AND ACCESSORIES

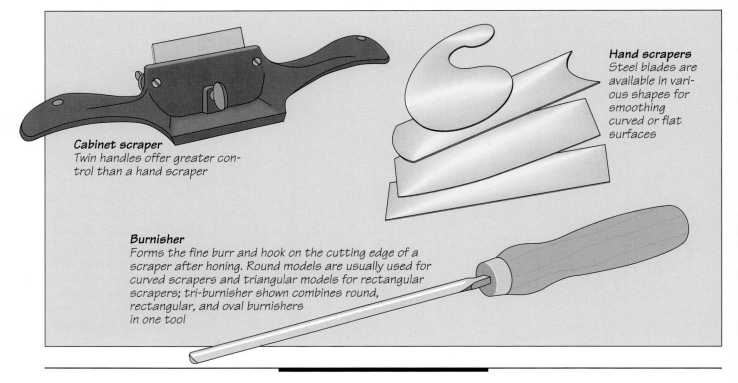

Hand scrapers
Steel blades are available in various shapes for smoothing curved or flat surfaces

Cabinet scraper
Twin handles offer greater control than a hand scraper

Burnisher
Forms the fine burr and hook on the cutting edge of a scraper after honing. Round models are usually used for curved scrapers and triangular models for rectangular scrapers; tri-burnisher shown combines round, rectangular, and oval burnishers in one tool

SHARPENING A HAND SCRAPER

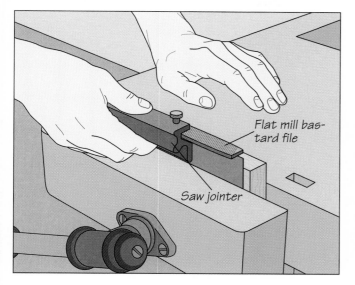

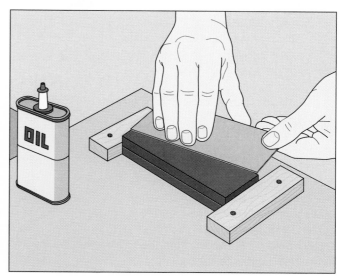

Flat mill bastard file

Saw jointer

1 Filing the edges square
Secure the scraper in a vise, edge up, with a wood block on one side to keep it rigid. Clamp a mill bastard file in a commercial saw jointer and press the jointer firmly against one side of the scraper. Exert moderate pressure as you make several passes back and forth along the edge of the tool *(above)* until the existing hook disappears and the edge is flat. Turn the scraper over in the vise and repeat the process for the other edge.

2 Honing the edges
Secure a combination sharpening stone fine-side up on a work surface with cleats and lubricate it. Pressing the scraper flat on the stone, rub each face with a circular motion *(above)* until any roughness produced by filing disappears. Next, hold the scraper upright and slide the edges back and forth diagonally across the stone until they are smooth with sharp corners. To finish, again slide the face lightly over the stone to remove any burrs.

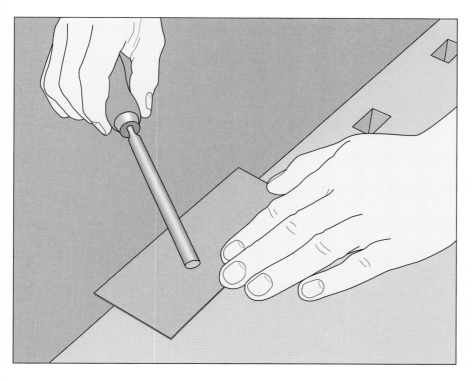

3 Burnishing the edges
Wipe a tiny amount of oil onto the edge of the scraper to reduce friction between the burnisher and the scraper. Start to form a hook on each cutting edge of the scraper by laying the scraper flat on a work surface with an edge extending off the table, then run the burnisher back and forth along the edge *(left)*, exerting strong downward pressure. Turn the scraper over and burnish the edge on the other face. Now burnish the other cutting edge the same way.

4 Turning the hook

Secure the scraper edge up in the vise and wipe a little more oil onto its edge. Holding the burnisher level, make a few passes along the edge in one direction until the edge swells slightly. Apply moderate pressure to turn the edge outward on one side *(right)*. Then hold the burnisher so that the handle is 10° to 15° above the horizontal and continue to burnish until the edge turns over into a hook. To form a hook on the other side of the edge *(below)*, repeat the process with the scraper turned around in the vise. The greater the pressure you apply, the bigger the hook. Turn the scraper over in the vise and turn the hooks on the opposite edge.

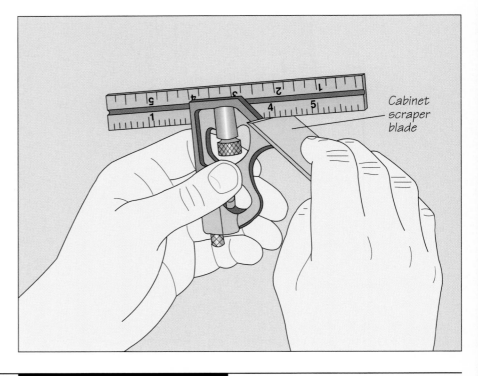

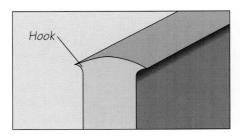

Hook

SHARPENING A CABINET SCRAPER

1 Filing the edge

Although its edge is beveled, a cabinet scraper is sharpened in much the same way as a hand scraper. Start by filing the bevel, then polish the bevel *(step 2)* and turn over a hook *(steps 3 and 4)*. Remove the blade from the cabinet scraper by loosening the thumbscrews holding it in place. Clamp the blade beveled-edge up in a vise between two wood pads. Then run a bastard mill file along the bevel, using a combination square periodically to check that the angle remains at 45° *(right)*.

Cabinet scraper blade

2 Polishing the bevel
Secure a sharpening stone to a work surface; in the illustration at left, a diamond stone is shown in a sharpening box. Lubricate the stone, then hold the scraper blade flat-side down and slide the blade in a circular pattern to remove any burr formed by filing. Next, turn the blade over so the bevel is flush on the stone and repeat to polish the bevel. A few passes should be sufficient. Use the combination square to help you maintain the bevel angle at 45° *(step 1)*.

3 Burnishing the cutting edge
Hold the scraper blade bevel down on a work surface with the cutting edge overhanging the table. Wipe some oil on the edge and, holding a burnisher at a slight angle to the blade, pass the rod back and forth across its flat edge *(below)*. Apply strong downward pressure forming a hook on the cutting edge.

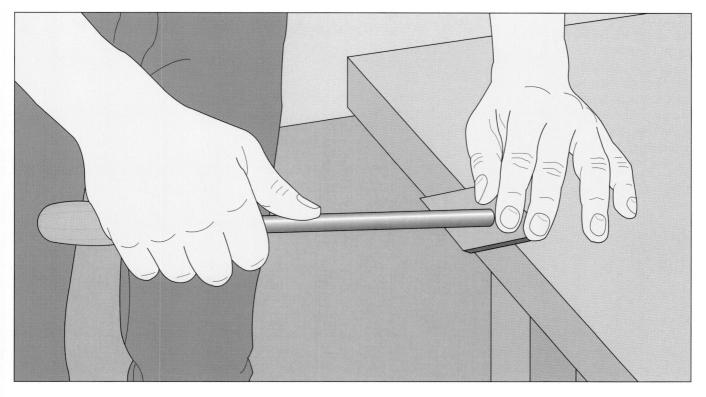

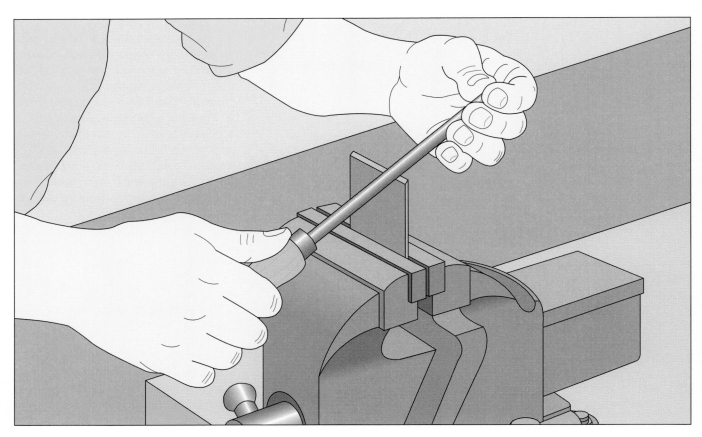

4 Forming the hook
Secure the blade bevel up in a machinist's vise and apply a little more oil on it. Holding the burnisher in both hands flush against the 45° bevel, pull the tool toward your body; maintain constant downward pressure *(above)*. Gradually tilt the handle of the burnisher until the rod is at angle of about 15° to the bevel. This will complete the hook on the cutting edge.

SHOP TIP

Maintaining the correct burnishing angle
Holding a burnisher at the proper angle is the key to burnishing the bevel of a cabinet scraper. As a visual guide, use a protractor and a square to mark a line at a 45° angle on the wall facing you when you do the burnishing. Locate the mark at eye level directly in line with your vise. As you pass the burnisher along the bevel, try to keep the rod parallel with the line on the wall.

45°

ROUGHING AND SHAPING TOOLS

The hand tools featured in this section of the chapter are as diverse as the individual tasks needed to work a standing tree into a piece of furniture. They range from rough to fine—axe to spokeshave, an implement most often used to whittle a workpiece to its final form.

For the sharpener, however, all these tools share one feature: They are single-bladed tools that rely on a correctly angled bevel to cut wood properly. The following pages will show you how to hone and polish each of the tools shown below. The first step in the process involves smoothing away defects and restoring the bevel on the blade, if the cutting edge requires it. This can be done on a bench grinder as you would a plane blade (*page 42*) or on a wet/dry grinder (*photo, right*). To prolong blade life, grind only what is required to restore the edge. Also, be careful not to overheat the blade; this can destroy the temper of the met-

al. One advantage of the wet/dry grinder is that you do not have to interrupt the grinding periodically to cool the blade. The water-bathed wheel automatically takes care of this concern.

A wet-dry grinder touches up an ax blade. To create a uniform bevel across the blade, it is important to hold the blade square to the grinding wheel and at a constant angle.

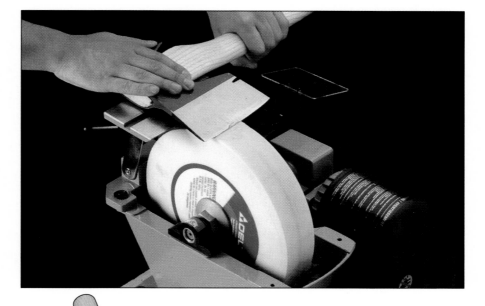

Inshave
A curved drawknife typically used to shape a workpiece after adzing; blade is beveled on outer side only

Adzes
Curved shaping tools for roughing out hollowed workpieces; hollowing adze (left) is beveled on outside edge

Spokeshaves
Metal flat-face model (top) smooths and shapes flat or convex surfaces; wooden spokeshave (bottom) is a traditional tool featuring a low cutting angle for shaping end grain. Both are pushed or pulled with the grain

Hewing hatchet
For rough shaping green wood; beveled on one side only for straight cutting

Drawknife
Used to debark green wood log sections and shape stock; blade is usually beveled on one side only for straight cutting

SHARPENING SPOKESHAVES

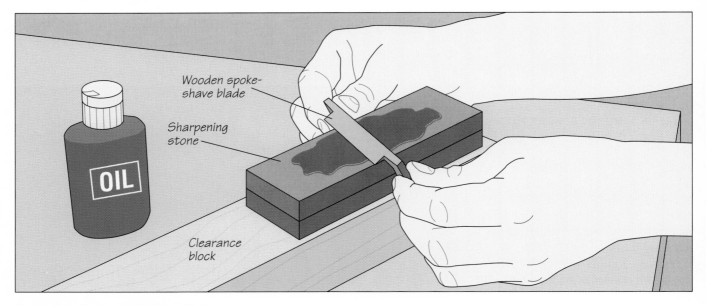

Sharpening a wooden spokeshave blade

Remove the blade from the handle by pinching the tangs that protrude through the handle and pushing them downward. For sharpening, the blade is held upside down from its usual cutting position—that is, with the tangs facing down rather than up. To prevent the tangs from catching on your work surface during sharpening, set your sharpening stone atop a wood block to provide the necessary clearance. Holding the blade by the tangs, set its bevel flat on the stone. Because the blade is longer than the width of the stone, hold the cutting edge diagonally as you slide the bevel back and forth on the stone. Repeat with the blade angled the other way. Repeat again with the blade held straight *(above)*. Once the sharpening is complete, turn the blade over and hone the flat side to remove the burr formed by the sharpening process.

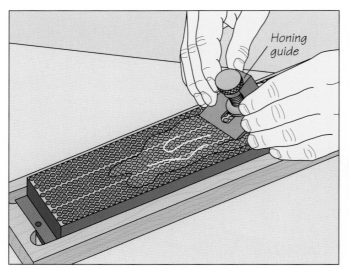

Honing a metal spokeshave blade

To remove the blade from the handle, loosen the screw in the middle of the handle. Set up a benchstone on a work surface; a water-lubricated diamond stone in a sharpening box is shown above. Install the blade in a commercial honing guide *(above, left)* and hone the cutting edge as you would a plane blade *(page 43)*. To flatten the sole of a flat-soled spokeshave, pass the sole back and forth along a medium-grit benchstone (above, right). Continue until the metal has uniform sheen.

SHARPENING A DRAWKNIFE

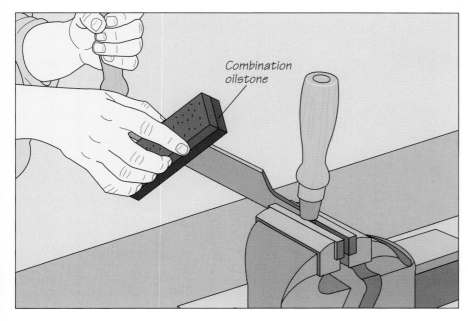

Combination oilstone

Honing a drawknife
Secure one handle of the drawknife in a machinist's vise with the blade level and the bevel facing up. Then lubricate a fine benchstone—in this case, a combination stone—and rub the stone along the length of the bevel, using a circular motion *(left)*. To hone a microbevel on the primary bevel, adjust the angle of the stone slightly. Finally, make a few passes on the flat side of the blade to remove any burr formed by sharpening.

SHARPENING AN INSHAVE

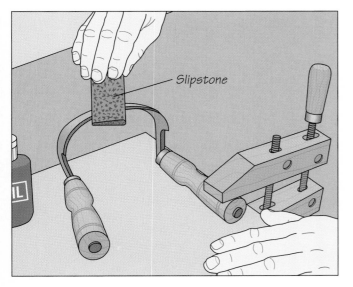

Slipstone

Honing an inshave
Clamp the inshave to a work surface so the cutting edge is facing up, as shown above. Use a slipstone to hone the edge. Start with a rough-grit stone and progress to a finer one. Work with a circular motion until a uniform shine develops on the blade. Give the flat side of the blade a few strokes to remove any burr. Once the blade is sharp, polish the bevel with a leather strop and polishing compound *(page 37)*, finishing with a few passes on the flat side of the blade to remove the burr. If the inshave has a knife-edge—beveled on both sides—hone the other side.

SHARPENING AN ADZE

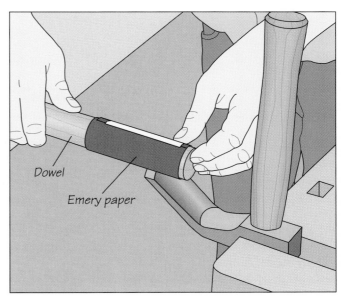

Dowel

Emery paper

Honing an adze
Secure the adze in a bench vise, as shown above. Wrap a sheet of emery paper around a dowel whose diameter closely matches the curve of the adze blade. Hone the cutting edge using a back-and-forth motion along the length of the bevel. Hone the flat side of the blade with a slipstone to remove any burr. If the adze has a knife-edge hone the other side.

POLISHING THE BLADE

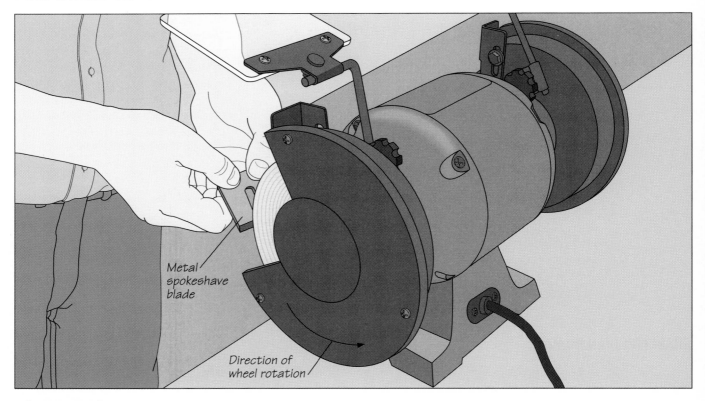

Metal
spokeshave
blade

Direction of
wheel rotation

Using a bench grinder
Once you have sharpened the blade of a roughing or shaping tool, polish the bevel and remove any burr formed by the process on the felt wheel of a bench grinder. For a metal spokeshave blade, impregnate the wheel with polishing compound and place the bevel of the blade on the trailing edge of the wheel *(above)*. Move the blade side to side to expose the entire bevel to the wheel. Buff the blade only enough to remove the burr, using a light touch to avoid rounding the edge. Run the whole length of the bevel back and forth across the wheel to polish it uniformly. Repeat on the flat side of the blade. Test the cutting edge for sharpness on a piece of softwood *(page 44)*.

SHOP TIP

Choosing a durable ax handle
Despite the availability of a variety of synthetic compounds, wooden-handled axes remain popular. They are light and strong, and feature a well-balanced feel. The strength of the handle depends on the orientation of the grain to the ax head. Choose an ax with a handle that has the grain running parallel to the cutting edge *(bottom)*; handles with the grain running perpendicular *(top)* to the face tend to break more easily.

BRACES AND BITS

Electric drills have largely superseded hand tools for boring holes in the modern woodshop. Nevertheless, most woodworkers still keep braces and hand drills handy, because these tools have unique capabilities not readily duplicated by power tools, such as working in tight quarters or boring a hole to a precise depth.

Maintaining these hand tools is mainly a question of keeping their moving parts clean and sharpening their bits. To clean a brace, unscrew the chuck shell and remove the jaws, as shown at right. Use the same cleaning procedure as you would for the parts of a bench plane *(page 40)*. The remaining pages of this chapter describe how to sharpen auger and spoon bits.

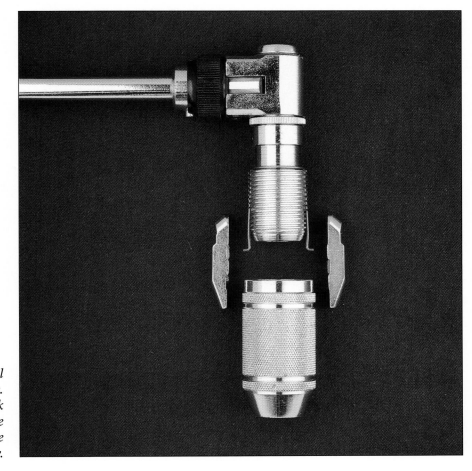

Cleaning the chuck is an essential element of maintaining a brace. The exploded view of a brace chuck in the photo at right shows the parts that require cleaning: the shell and the two-piece jaw.

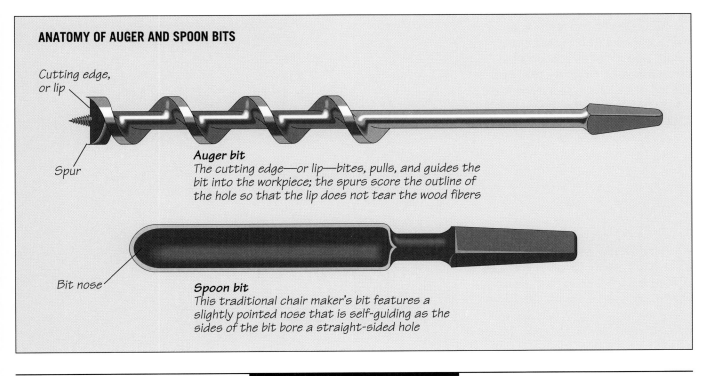

ANATOMY OF AUGER AND SPOON BITS

Cutting edge, or lip

Spur

Auger bit
The cutting edge—or lip—bites, pulls, and guides the bit into the workpiece; the spurs score the outline of the hole so that the lip does not tear the wood fibers

Bit nose

Spoon bit
This traditional chair maker's bit features a slightly pointed nose that is self-guiding as the sides of the bit bore a straight-sided hole

SHARPENING AN AUGER BIT

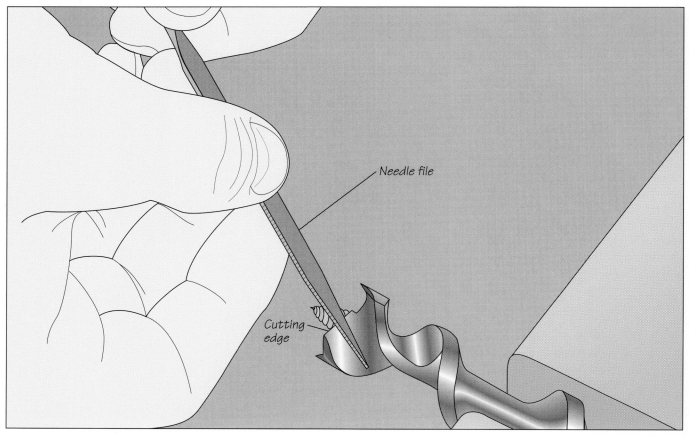

Needle file

Cutting edge

Spur

1 Filing the cutting edge

Secure the bit in a bench vise, then use a needle file to sharpen the cutting edge. (You can also use a specialized auger bit file for the job.) Hold the file on the leading edge and make a few strokes along the surface. Repeat with the other cutting edge.

2 Filing the spur

Position the bit upright in the vise. Holding the file flush against the inside edge of one spur, make several strokes across the surface (right) until you produce an even shine on the spur. Repeat with the other spur.

3 Removing burrs from the spurs
Holding a very fine diamond hone on a work surface, slide the outside edge of one of the bit spurs on the stone to remove any burr formed by sharpening *(right)*. (You can also use a piece of very fine emery cloth.) Work with a light touch and use only enough strokes to remove the burr, or you risk reducing the bit diameter. Repeat with the other spur.

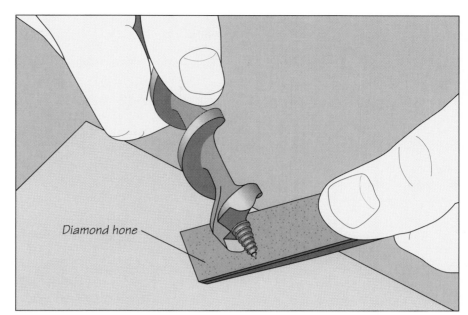

Diamond hone

SHARPENING AN SPOON BIT

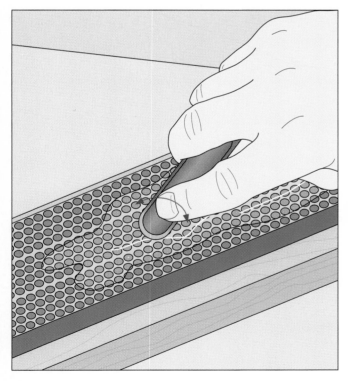

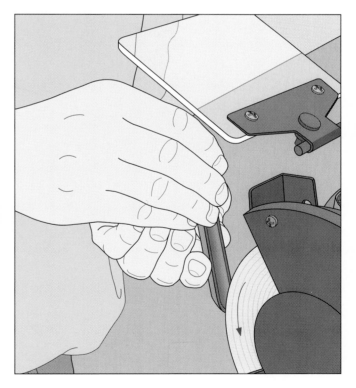

Sharpening a spoon bit

Spoon bits can be sharpened easily on a benchstone. In the illustration above, at left, a diamond stone in its own sharpening box is shown. Holding the outside of the bit's nose on the stone, rock the bit across the surface with a semicircular motion. Hold the bit at the same angle throughout to ensure that the nose is honed uniformly. Once the sharpening is completed, polish both sides of the nose on the felt wheel of a bench grinder. Impregnate the wheel with polishing compound and, holding the bit vertically, lightly touch the front of the nose to the wheel *(above, right)*. Repeat with the back side.

SHARPENING POWER TOOL BLADES AND BITS

Designed to replace the metal guide blocks supplied with most band saws, heat-resistant guide blocks can help prolong blade life. Made from a graphite-impregnated resin that is its own lubricant, these nonmetallic blocks last longer than metal blocks and can be set closer to the blade, allowing more accurate and controlled cuts.

Like any cutting or shaping tool, a power tool with a dull blade or bit cannot perform well. A dull drill bit will tend to skate off a workpiece, rather than biting cleanly into the wood. A saw blade or router bit with blunted cutting edges may burn stock. And wood that is surfaced by a jointer or planer with unsharpened knives may be difficult to glue up or finish.

In addition to cutting and shaping properly, well-sharpened blades and bits offer other benefits, including reduced wear and tear on motors, less operator fatigue, and longer life for the blades and bits themselves. Manufacturers of power tool blades and bits generally recommend sending their products to a professional sharpening service. However, the job can often be done in the workshop. This chapter will show you how to sharpen a wide variety of power tool blades and bits, from router bits and shaper cutters *(page 62)* to jointer and planer knives *(page 79)*. In a pinch, even a broken band saw blade can be soldered together *(page 76)*.

Still, there are times when you should turn to a professional, particularly if blades and bits have chipped edges or have lost their temper as a result of overgrinding. Some router bits also must be precisely balanced, something that is difficult to achieve in the shop. As a rule of thumb, it is a good idea to send out your bits and blades to a sharpening service periodically, or every second time they need a major sharpening. Once you have sharpened an edge properly, it should last for a long time—the occasional honing is all that it takes to maintain it.

The pages that follow cover the basic techniques for sharpening power tool blades and bits in the shop. With a little practice and the right accessories, you can keep the cutting edges of your blades and bits razor-sharp. But remember that a keen edge always starts with the quality of the steel itself; for long life and ease of sharpening, always choose bits and blades made from the best steel.

A twist bit is sharpened on a bench grinder with the help of a commercial grinding jig that holds the bit at the proper angle. Originally designed for the metalworking industry, twist bits took their place in woodworking as the use of power tools grew. They need periodic sharpening to bore holes cleanly and accurately.

A GALLERY OF BLADES AND BITS

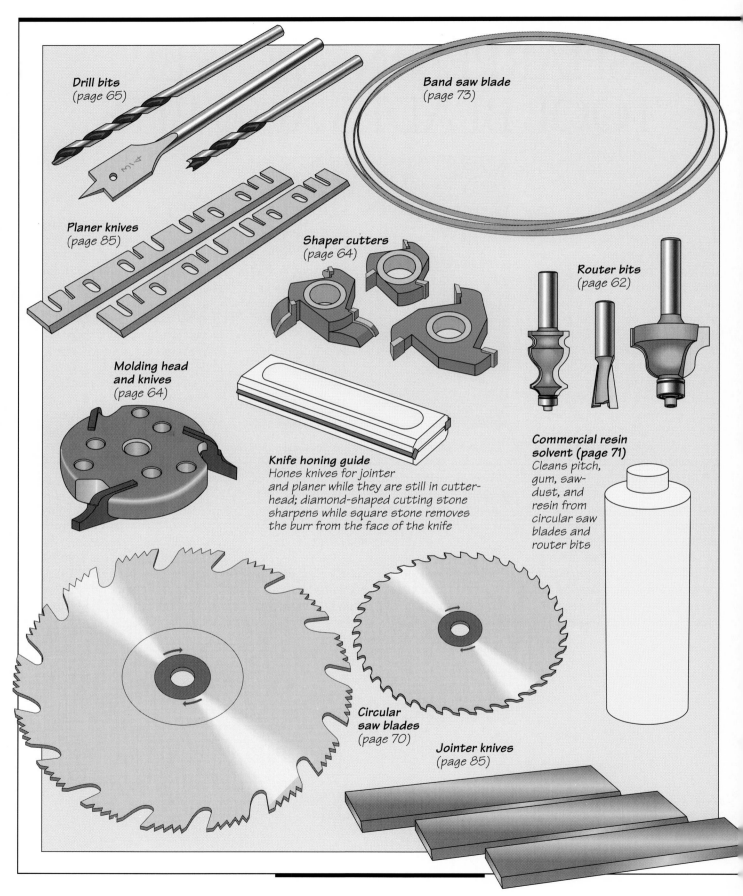

Drill bits
(page 65)

Band saw blade
(page 73)

Planer knives
(page 85)

Shaper cutters
(page 64)

Router bits
(page 62)

**Molding head
and knives**
(page 64)

Knife honing guide
Hones knives for jointer
and planer while they are still in cutterhead; diamond-shaped cutting stone
sharpens while square stone removes
the burr from the face of the knife

**Commercial resin
solvent (page 71)**
Cleans pitch,
gum, saw-
dust, and
resin from
circular saw
blades and
router bits

**Circular
saw blades**
(page 70)

Jointer knives
(page 85)

TOOLS AND ACCESSORIES FOR SHARPENING

Drill bit grinding attachment (page 58)
Holds ⅛- to ¾-inch-diameter twist bits for sharpening; mounted to work surface and used with a bench grinder

Router bit sharpener
A boron-carbide stone used to sharpen carbon steel, high-speed steel, and carbide-tipped router bits; gives a finer finish than diamond files of equal grit. Handle features magnifying lens for checking sharpness

Drill bit-sharpening jig (page 66)
Powered by an electric drill, this jig sharpens high-speed steel twist bits and carbide masonry bits up to ½ inch in diameter; holder secures bit at proper depth and angle against sharpening stone inside jig

Circular saw blade-setting jig (page 72)
Clamped in bench vise to joint and set the teeth of circular saws up to 12 inches in diameter. Blade is locked in jig and rotated against file to joint teeth; teeth are set by tapping them with a hammer against mandrel

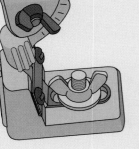

Knife-setting jigs (page 79)
Magnetic jig used to hold jointer or planer knives at the correct height for installation in the machine. Jigs for planer (below) are used in pairs for knives up to 20 inches long; jig for jointer (right) sets knives up to 8 inches in length, and can be extended with a third bar for knives up to 14 inches long

Jointer/planer-knife sharpening jig (page 79)
Used to sharpen jointer and planer knives; knife is clamped in jig and rear screw adjusts to hold knife at proper angle against a bench stone

Circular saw blade-sharpening jig (page 72)
Mounted on workbench to sharpen circular saw blades after grinding and setting; blade is held in jig while taper file is drawn across the teeth at the proper pitch and angle

ROUTER BITS AND SHAPER CUTTERS

Secured in a bench vise, one of the cutting edges of a shaper cutter receives its final sharpening with a fine diamond hone. The process is a two-step operation, beginning with a medium hone (far left). Because they operate at high speeds, dull router bits and shaper cutters overheat quickly. Cutters that are properly sharpened make smoother, more accurate cuts.

SHARPENING A NON-PILOTED ROUTER BIT

Sharpening the inside faces

Clean any pitch, gum, or sawdust off the bit with a commercial resin solvent *(page 71)*, then use a ceramic or diamond sharpening file to hone the inside faces of the bit's cutting edges. A coarse-grit file is best if a lot of material needs to be removed; use a finer-grit file for a light touch-up. Holding the inside face of one cutting edge flat against the abrasive surface, rub it back and forth *(right)*. Repeat with the other cutting edge. Hone both inside faces equally to maintain the balance of the bit. Take care not to file the bevel behind the cutting edge.

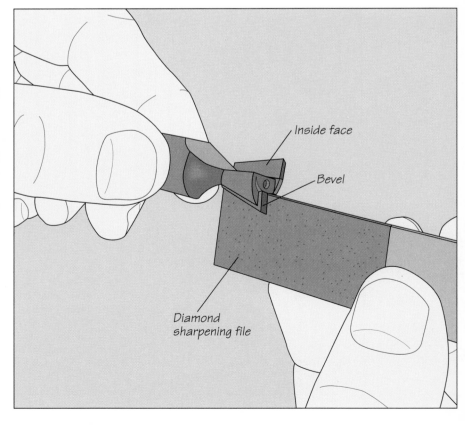

Inside face

Bevel

Diamond sharpening file

SHARPENING A PILOTED ROUTER BIT

Hex wrench

Pilot bearing

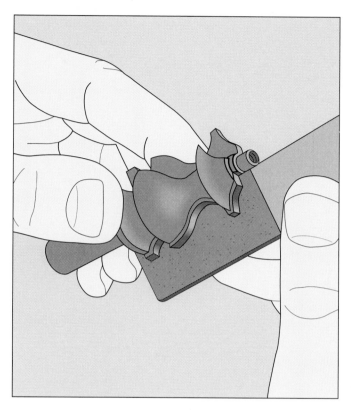

1 Removing the pilot bearing
Before you can sharpen a piloted router bit, you need to remove the pilot bearing. Use a hex wrench to loosen the bearing *(above)*.

2 Sharpening the bit
Sharpen the bit with a ceramic or diamond sharpening file as you would a non-piloted bit *(page 62)*; then re-install the bearing with the hex wrench. If the bearing does not rotate smoothly, spray a little bearing lubricant on it. If it is worn out or damaged, replace it.

SHOP TIP

A storage rack for shaper cutters
Shaper cutters are often sold in cumbersome packaging that can contribute to clutter. Organize your shaper bits with a shop-made storage rack like the one shown here. The rack will keep the cutters visible and accessible. Drill a series of holes in a board and glue dowels in the holes to hold the cutters. To prevent the cutting edges from nicking each other, use your largest-diameter cutter as a guide to spacing the dowel holes. If you plan to hang the rack on a wall, bore the holes at a slight angle so that the cutters will not slip off the dowels.

MOLDING KNIVES

SHARPENING MOLDING KNIVES

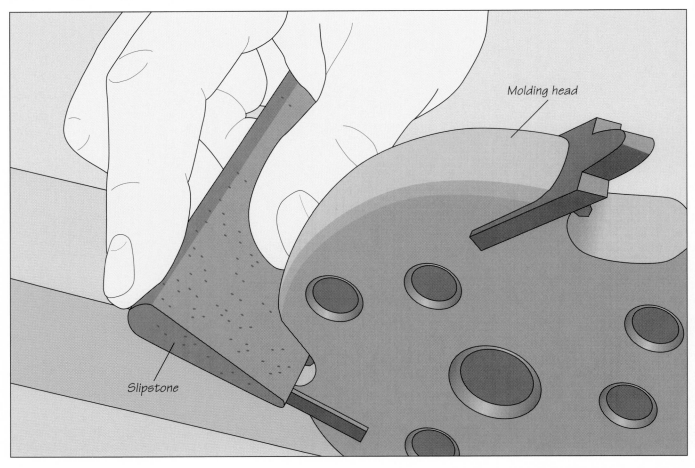

Molding head

Slipstone

Sharpening molding knives

The cutting edges of table saw or radial arm saw molding knives are easy to touch up or sharpen while they are mounted in the molding head. Clamp the head in a bench vise with one of the knives clear of the bench, then use a slipstone *(above)* to hone its inside face as you would a router bit *(page 62)*. Reposition the head in the vise to hone the remaining knives. Use the same number of strokes to hone each knife so that you remove an equal amount of metal from them all, and maintain their identical shapes and weights. An alternative method involves removing the knives with a hex wrench *(right)* and sharpening them on a flat oilstone.

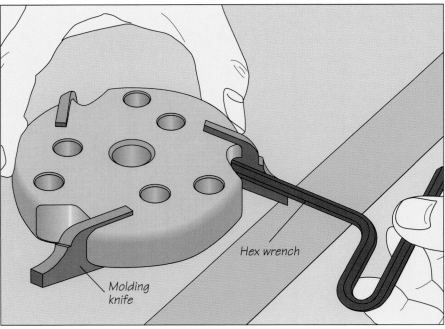

Hex wrench

Molding knife

DRILL BITS

SHARPENING TWIST BITS

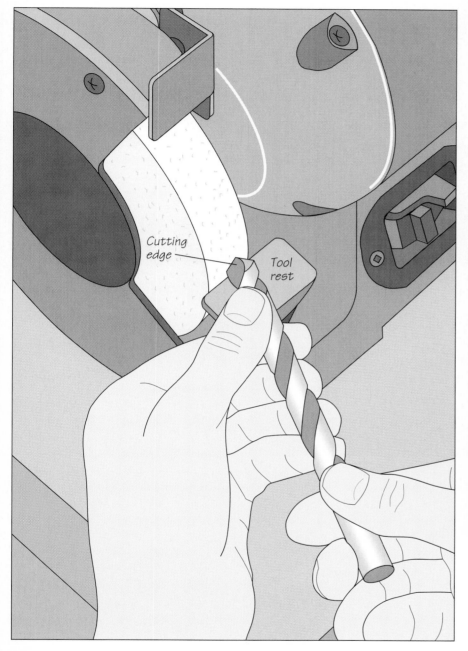

Cutting edge

Tool rest

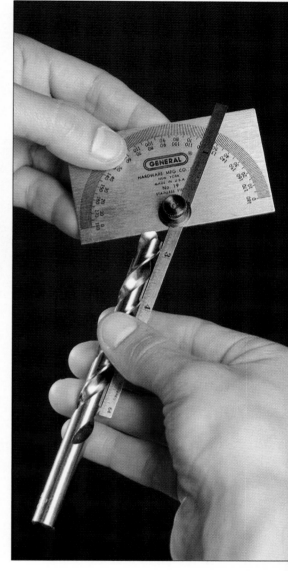

To bore clean holes, the cutting edges of twist bits should be angled at about 60°. As you sharpen a bit, periodically check the angle with a protractor. Butt one of the cutting edges against the base of the protractor and swivel the arm flush against the side of the bit.

Using a bench grinder

Holding the bit between the index finger and thumb of one hand, set it on the grinder's tool rest and advance it toward the wheel until your index finger contacts the tool rest. Tilt the shaft of the bit down and to the left so that one of the cutting edges, or lips, is square to the wheel *(above)*. Rotate the bit clockwise to grind the lip evenly. Periodically check the angle of the cutting edge, as shown in the photo at right, and try to maintain the angle at about 60°. Repeat for the second cutting edge. To keep bits sharp, use them at the speed recommended by the manufacturer. Wipe them occasionally with oil to prevent rust.

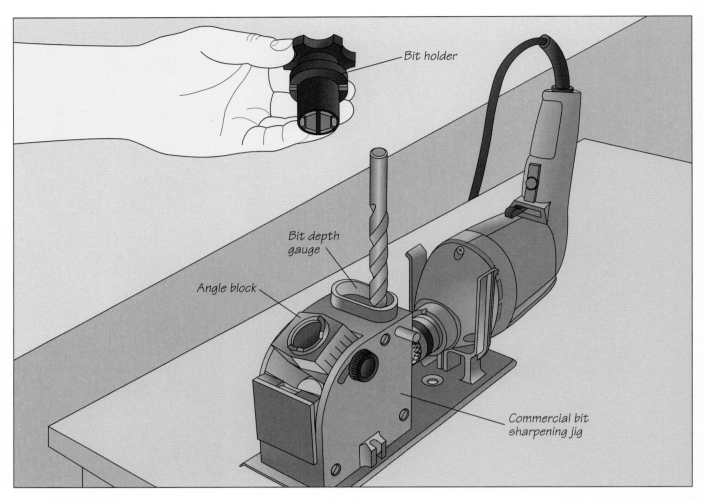

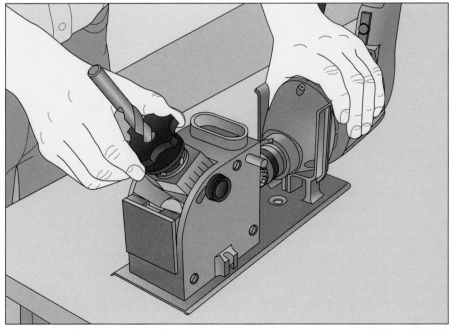

Using a commercial jig

Set up the jig following the manufacturer's instructions. For the model shown, secure an electric drill to the jig; the drill will rotate the sharpening stone inside the device. Adjust the angle block to the appropriate angle for the bit to be sharpened and insert the bit in the depth gauge. The gauge will enable you to secure the bit at the correct height in the holder. Fit the bit holder over the bit *(above)* and then use it to remove the bit from the gauge. Now secure the bit and holder to the angle block. Turn on the drill and, holding it steady, slowly rotate the bit holder a full 360° against the stone inside the jig *(right)*. Apply light pressure; too much force will overheat the bit.

SHARPENING FORSTNER BITS

1 Grinding the inside bevel
To touch up a Forstner bit, true the top edge of the bit's rim with a file, removing any nicks. If the beveled edges of the cutting spurs inside the rim are uneven, grind them using an electric drill fitted with a rotary grinding attachment. Secure the bit in a bench vise as shown and grind the edges until they are all uniform *(right)*.

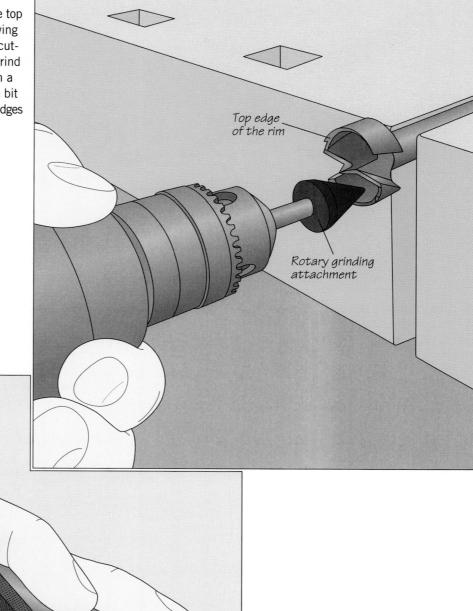

Top edge
of the rim

Rotary grinding
attachment

Chip
lifter

2 Sharpening the chip lifters
Use a single-cut mill bastard file to lightly file the inside faces of the cutters. Hold the file flat against one of the cutters—also known as chip lifters—and make a few strokes along the surface *(left)*. Repeat with the other cutter. Finish the job by honing the beveled edges inside the rim with a slipstone.

HONING MULTI-SPUR BITS

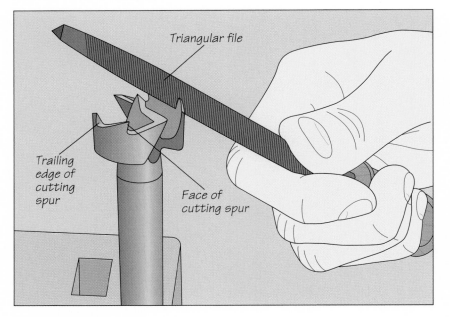

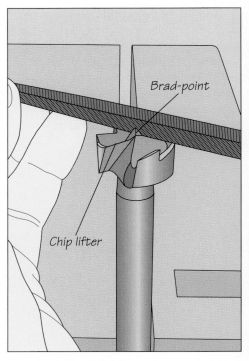

1 Filing the cutting spurs

Secure the bit upright in a bench vise and use a triangular file to hone the leading edge, or face, of each spur *(above)*. File with each push stroke, towards the bit's brad point, tilting the handle of the file down slightly. Then file the trailing edge, or back, of each spur the same way. File all the spurs by the same amount so that they remain at the same height. Make sure you do not over-file the cutting spurs; they are designed to be ⅓₂ inch longer than the chip lifters.

2 Filing the brad point

File the chip lifters as you would those of a Forstner bit *(page 67)*. Then, file the brad-point until it is sharp *(above)*.

SHARPENING BRAD-POINT BITS

1 Filing the chip lifters

Clamp the bit upright in a bench vise and file the inside faces of the two chip lifters as you would those of a Forstner bit *(page 67)*. For a brad-point bit, however, use a triangular needle file *(right)*, honing until each cutting edge is sharp and each chip lifter is flat.

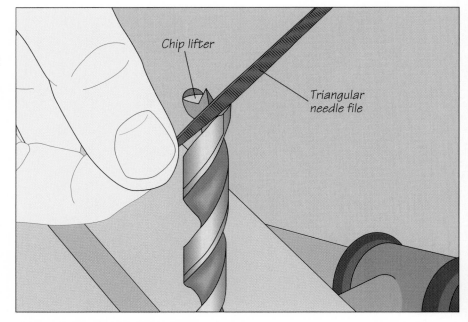

2 Filing the cutting spurs

Use the needle file to hone the inside faces of the bit's two cutting spurs. Hold the tool with both hands and file towards the brad-point until each spur is sharp *(right)*.

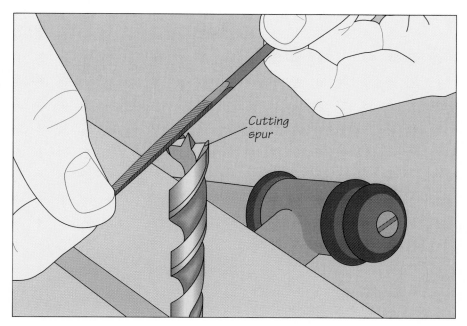

Cutting spur

HONING SPADE BITS

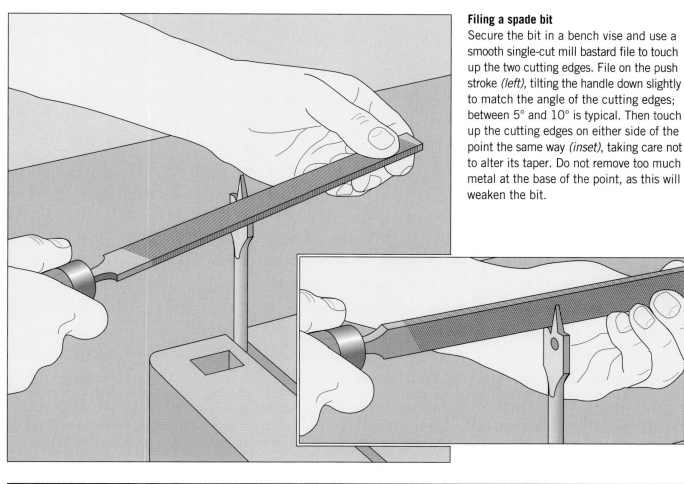

Filing a spade bit

Secure the bit in a bench vise and use a smooth single-cut mill bastard file to touch up the two cutting edges. File on the push stroke *(left)*, tilting the handle down slightly to match the angle of the cutting edges; between 5° and 10° is typical. Then touch up the cutting edges on either side of the point the same way *(inset)*, taking care not to alter its taper. Do not remove too much metal at the base of the point, as this will weaken the bit.

CIRCULAR SAW BLADES

CHANGING TABLE SAW BLADES

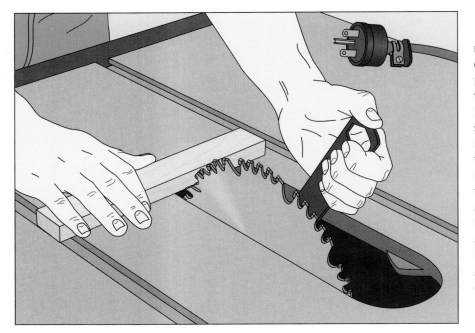

The commercial blade carrier shown above is a handy storage device that will protect your circular saw blades from damage and make it easier to transport them. This model accommodates up to ten 10-inch blades.

1 Removing a blade
Working at the front of the table, remove the insert and wedge a piece of scrap wood under a blade tooth to prevent the blade from turning. Use the wrench supplied with the saw to loosen the arbor nut *(left)*. (Most table saw arbors have reverse threads; the nut is loosened in a clockwise direction.) Finish loosening the nut by hand, making sure that it does not fall into the machine. Carefully lift the blade and washer off the arbor. Carbide-tipped blades are best sharpened professionally; but high-speed steel models can be sharpened in the shop *(page 72)*. A worn or damaged blade should be discarded and replaced.

2 Installing a blade
Slide the blade onto the arbor with its teeth pointing in the direction of blade rotation (toward the front of the table). Insert the flange and nut and start tightening by hand. To finish tightening, grip the saw blade with a rag and use the wrench supplied with the saw *(above)*. Do not use a piece of wood as a wedge, as this could result in overtightening the nut.

CHANGING PORTABLE CIRCULAR SAW BLADES

Removing a portable circular saw blade

Set the saw on its side on a work surface with the blade housing facing up. Retract the lower blade guard and, gripping the blade with a rag, loosen the arbor nut with the wrench supplied with the saw *(right)*. Remove the nut and the outer washer, then slide the blade from the arbor. As with table saw blades, carbide-tipped blades should be sent out for sharpening, but high-speed steel types can be sharpened in the shop. To install a blade, place it on the arbor with its teeth pointing in the direction of blade rotation. Install the washer and the nut, and tighten them by hand. Holding the blade with the rag, use the wrench to give the nut an additional quarter turn. Do not overtighten.

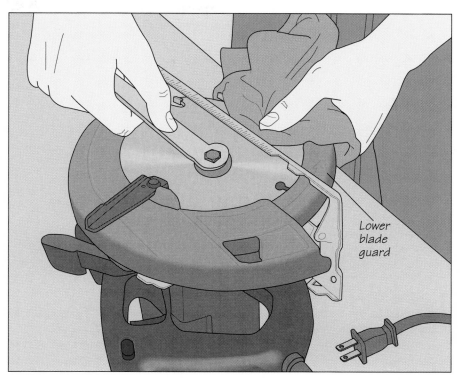

Lower blade guard

CLEANING CIRCULAR SAW BLADES

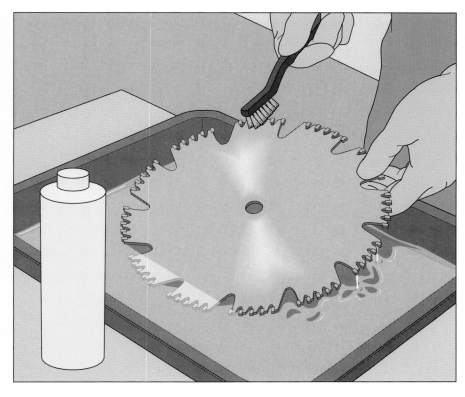

Soaking the blade

Clean the blade using a commercial resin solvent. (Commercial oven cleaner, turpentine, or a solution of hot water with ammonia can also be used.) For stubborn pitch and gum deposits, soak the blade in the cleaning agent in a shallow pan and use a brass-bristled brush to clean the teeth *(left)*.

SHARPENING CIRCULAR SAW BLADES

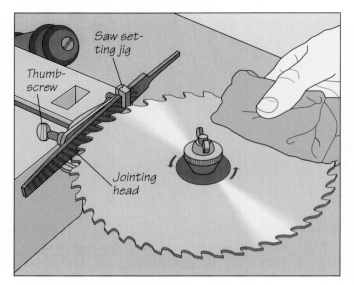

1 Jointing the teeth
To sharpen the teeth of a circular saw blade, install the blade in a commercial saw-setting jig following the manufacturer's instructions. For the model shown, the blade teeth should be pointing counterclockwise. Install the jointing head on the jig, butting its file up against the saw teeth. Then tighten the thumbscrew until the teeth drag against the file. To joint the teeth so they are all the same length, clamp the jig in a bench vise and rotate the blade against the file clockwise *(above)*. After each rotation, tighten the thumbscrew slightly and repeat until the tip of each tooth has been filed flat.

2 Setting the teeth
Remove the jointing head from the jig and install the setting head. Also remove the jig from the vise and set it on the benchtop. Adjust the head for the appropriate amount of set, or bend. Using a pin punch and ball-peen hammer, lightly strike every second tooth against the setting head *(above)*. Remove the blade and reverse the position of the setting head. Reinstall the blade with the teeth pointing in the opposite direction, and repeat for the teeth you skipped, again striking every second tooth.

3 Sharpening the teeth
Once the saw teeth have been jointed and set, file them using a commercial saw-sharpening jig. Mount the jig to a workbench and install the blade loosely on the jig so the blade turns. Following the manufacturer's instructions, rotate the triangular file in the file holder and adjust the guide arm to match the required pitch and angle of the saw teeth. Starting with a tooth that is pointing to the right, file the cutting edge by sliding the file holder along the top of the jig *(right)*. Rotate the blade counterclockwise, skipping one tooth, and repeat. Sharpen all the right-pointing teeth the same way. Adjust the triangular file and the guide arm to work on the left-pointing teeth and repeat, sharpening all the teeth you skipped.

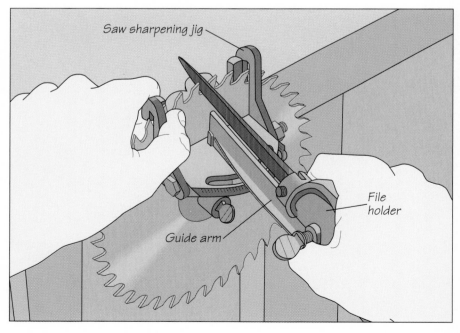

Secured between two wood blocks in a bench vise, the teeth of a band saw blade are sharpened with a triangular file. Band saw blades can also be honed while they are installed on the machine. The teeth should be sharpened periodically and set after every three to five sharpenings. In fact, a properly honed and set band saw blade will perform better than a brand new one.

SHARPENING A BAND SAW BLADE

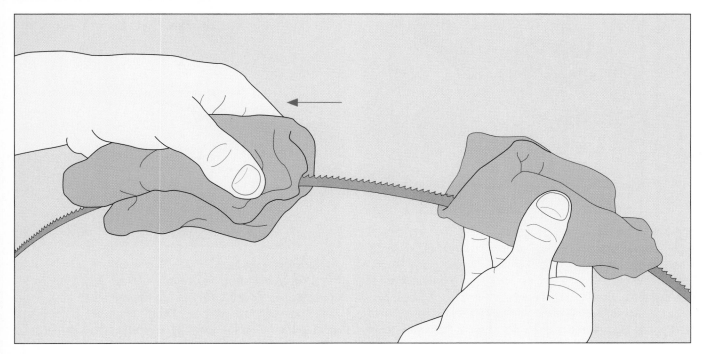

1 Cleaning the blade

Before sharpening a band saw blade, remove sawdust and wood chips from it. Make sure you release the blade tension first before slipping the blade off the wheels. Then, holding the blade between two clean rags *(above)*, pull it away in the direction opposite its normal rotation to avoid snagging the cutting edges in the material.

2 Installing the blade for sharpening

You can sharpen a band saw blade either on a bench vise *(photo, page 73)* or on the machine. To install the blade on the band saw for sharpening, mount it with the teeth pointing in the direction opposite their cutting position—that is, facing up instead of down. Turn the blade inside out and guide it through the table slot *(right)*, holding it with the teeth facing you and pointing up. Slip the blade between the guide blocks and in the throat column slot, then center it on the wheels. Make sure the blade guide assembly is raised as high above the table as it will go.

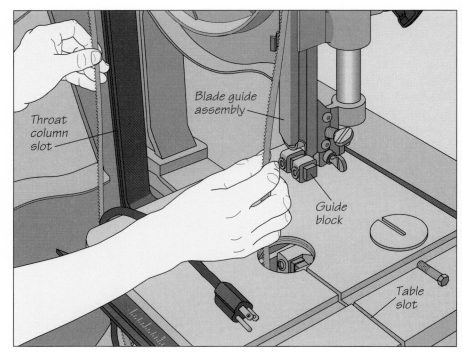

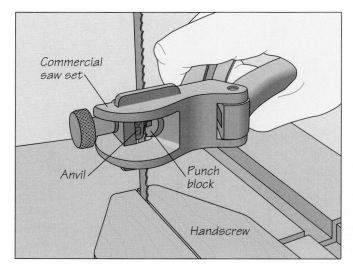

3 Setting the blade

If the teeth need to be set, adjust a commercial saw set to the same number of teeth per inch as the band saw blade. Secure the blade in a handscrew and clamp the handscrew to the saw table. Starting at the handscrew-end of the blade, position the first tooth that is bent to the right between the anvil and punch block of the saw set and squeeze the handle to set the tooth *(above)*. Work your way up to the guide assembly, setting all the teeth that are bent to the right. Then turn the saw set over and repeat for the leftward-bent teeth. Continue setting all the blade teeth section by section. To ensure you do not omit any teeth, mark each section you work on with chalk.

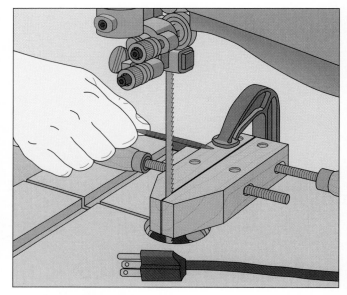

4 Sharpening the blade

Sharpen the teeth the same way you set them, working on one blade section at a time. Hold a triangular file at a 90° angle to the blade and sharpen each tooth that is set to the right, guiding the file in the same direction that the tooth is set *(above)*. Then sharpen the leftward-bent teeth the same way. Use the same number of strokes on each tooth. Once all the teeth have been sharpened, remove the blade, turn it inside out and reinstall it for cutting, with the teeth pointing down. Tension and track the blade *(page 123.)*

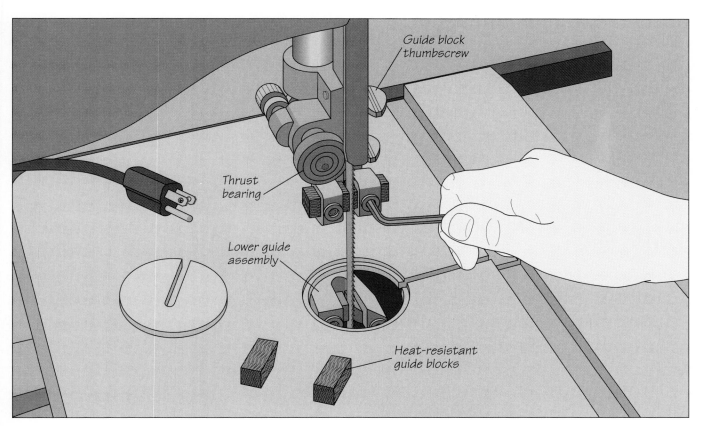

Guide block
thumbscrew

Thrust
bearing

Lower guide
assembly

Heat-resistant
guide blocks

SHOP TIP

Rounding a band saw blade
To help prevent a new band saw
blade from binding in
the kerf of curved
cuts, use a silicon-
carbide stone without
oil to round its back
edge, as shown here.
Attach the stone to
a shop-made handle.
Tension and track the
blade (page 123), then
turn on the saw. Wearing
safety goggles, hold the stone
against the back of the blade and
slowly pivot the stone. Turn off the saw after a few minutes.
In addition to rounding the back of the blade, the stone will
smooth any bumps where the blade ends are welded together.

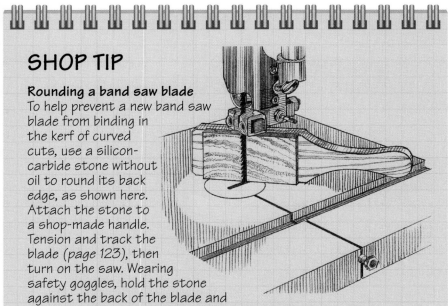

Installing heat-resistant guide blocks
Replacing your band saw's standard guide
blocks with heat-resistant blocks will
lengthen blade life and promote more
accurate and controlled cuts. Remove the
original blocks by using a hex wrench to
loosen the setscrews securing them to the
upper guide assembly *(above)*. Slip out
the old blocks and insert the replace-
ments. Pinch the blocks together with
your thumb and index finger until they
almost touch the blade. (You can also
use a slip of paper to set the space between the guide blocks and the blade).
Tighten the setscrews. The front edges
of the guide blocks should be just behind
the blade gullets. To reposition the blocks,
loosen their thumbscrew and turn their
adjustment knob to advance or retract
the blocks. Tighten the thumbscrew and
repeat the process for the guide assembly located below the table.

REPAIRING A BROKEN BAND SAW BLADE

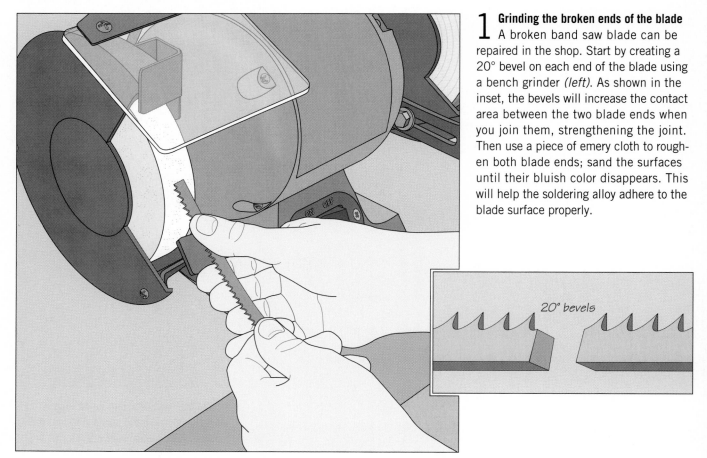

1 **Grinding the broken ends of the blade**
A broken band saw blade can be repaired in the shop. Start by creating a 20° bevel on each end of the blade using a bench grinder *(left)*. As shown in the inset, the bevels will increase the contact area between the two blade ends when you join them, strengthening the joint. Then use a piece of emery cloth to roughen both blade ends; sand the surfaces until their bluish color disappears. This will help the soldering alloy adhere to the blade surface properly.

20° bevels

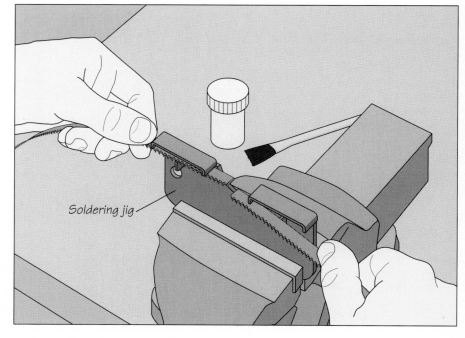

Soldering jig

2 **Setting up the blade in the soldering jig**
Secure a commercial soldering jig in a machinist's vise. Next, use a brush to spread flux on the beveled ends of the blade and ½ inch in from each end. Position the blade in the jig so the two beveled ends are in contact *(right)*. Make sure the blade is tight and straight in the jig.

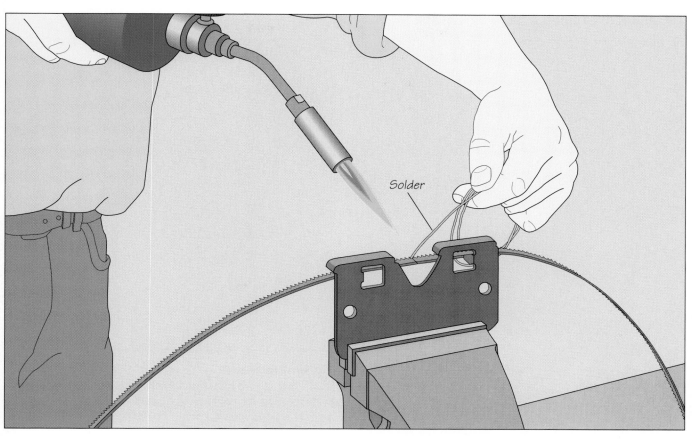

Solder

3 Soldering the blade ends

Heat the joint with a propane torch, then unroll a length of the solder and touch the tip to the joint—not to the flame. Continue heating the joint *(above)* until the solder covers the joint completely. Turn off the torch and let the joint cool.

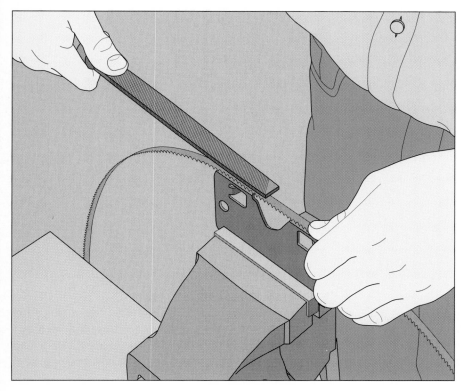

4 Filing the joint

Once the joint has cooled, remove the blade from the jig and wash off the flux with warm water. If there is an excess of solder on the blade, file it off carefully with a single-cut bastard mill file *(left)* until the joint is no thicker than the rest of the blade. If the joint separates, reheat it to melt the solder, pull it apart, and repeat steps 2 through 4.

FOLDING AND STORING A BAND SAW BLADE

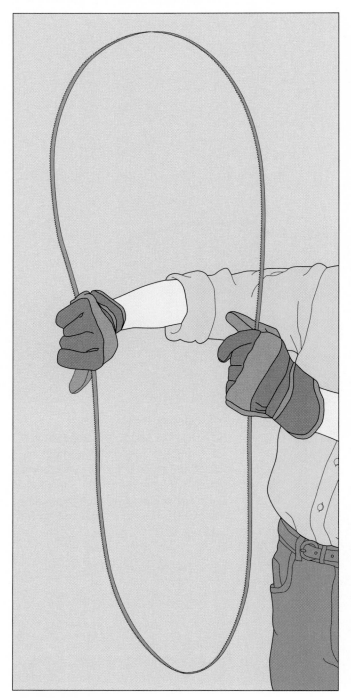

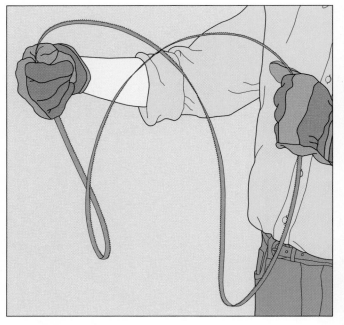

2 Twisting the blade
Pressing your right thumb firmly against the blade, twist it by pivoting your right hand upward. The blade will begin to form two loops *(above)*.

1 Holding the blade
Before storing a band saw blade, remove any rust from it with steel wool and wipe it with an oily rag. Then, wearing safety goggles and gloves, grasp the blade with the teeth facing away from you; point your left thumb up and your right thumb down *(above)*.

3 Coiling the blade
Without pausing or releasing the blade, keep rotating it in the same direction while pivoting your left hand in the opposite direction. The blade will coil again, forming a third loop *(above)*. Secure the blade with string, pipe cleaners, or plastic twist ties.

JOINTER AND PLANER KNIVES

A pair of magnetic jigs holds a planer knife at the correct height in the cutterhead, allowing the knife to be fixed in place accurately. Such jigs take the guesswork out of the trickiest phase of sharpening planer knives—installing them properly. Periodic sharpening of planer knives is essential. Stock that is surfaced by dull knives is difficult to glue and does not accept finishes well. A similar jig is available for setting jointer knives.

HONING JOINTER KNIVES

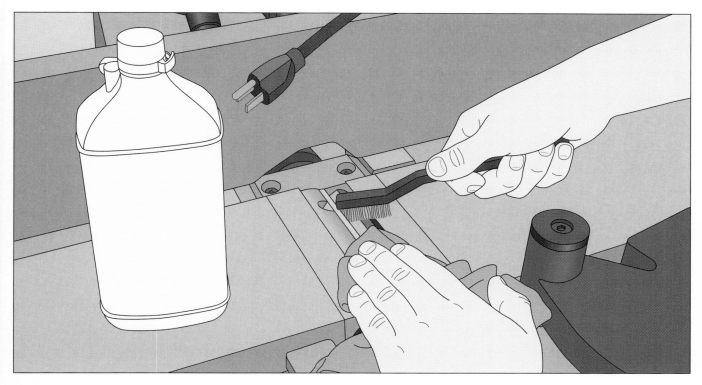

1 Cleaning the knives
Jointer knives can be honed while they are in the cutterhead. Start by cleaning them. Shift the fence away from the tables and move the guard out of the way. Making sure the jointer is unplugged, rotate the cutterhead with a stick until one of the knives is at the highest point in its rotation. Then, holding the cutterhead steady with one hand protected by a rag, use a small brass-bristled brush soaked in solvent to clean the knife *(above)*. Repeat for the other knives.

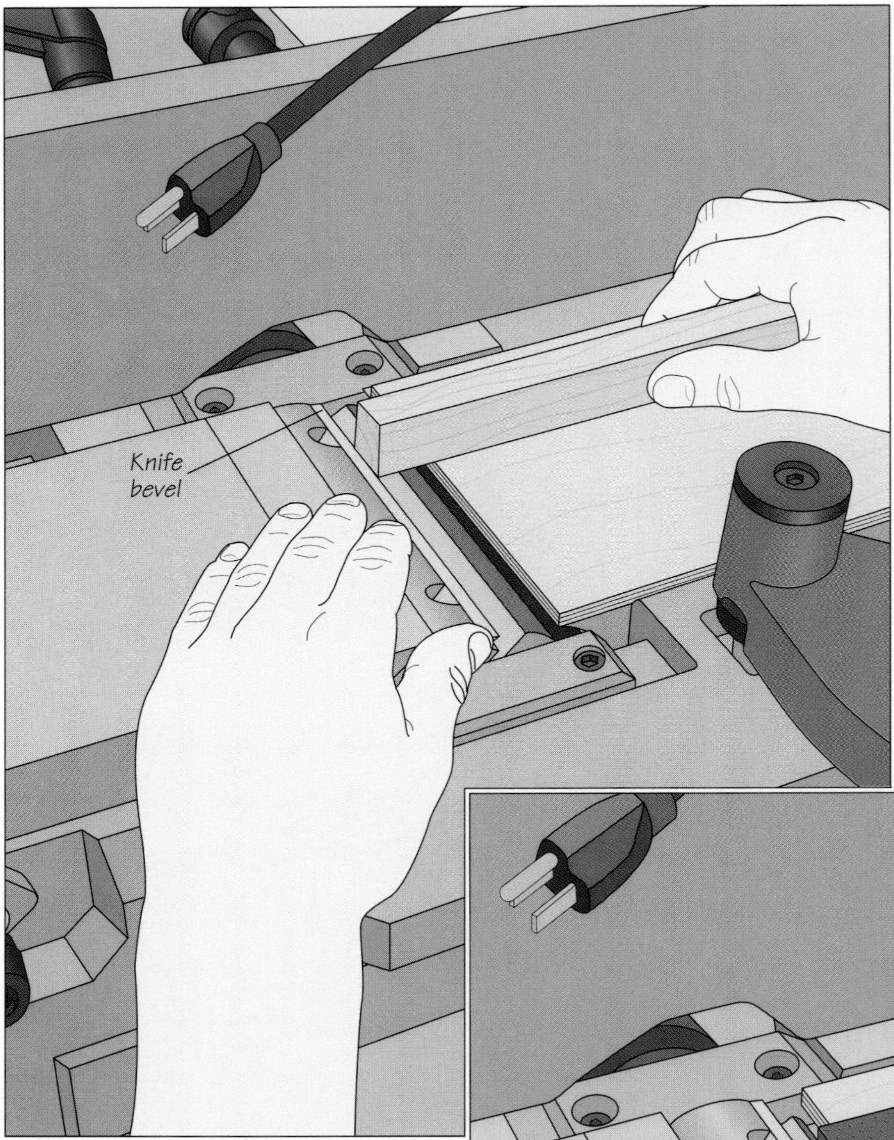

2 Aligning the infeed table with the knives

Cut a piece of ¼-inch plywood to the width of the jointer's infeed table and secure it to the table with double-faced tape. The plywood will protect the table from scratches when you hone the knives. Next, adjust the infeed table so that the beveled edge of the knives is at the same level as the top of the plywood. Set a straight board on the plywood and across the cutterhead and, holding the cutterhead steady with the beveled edge of one knife parallel to the table, lower the infeed table until the bottom of the board contacts the bevel *(left)*. Use a wood shim to wedge the cutterhead in place.

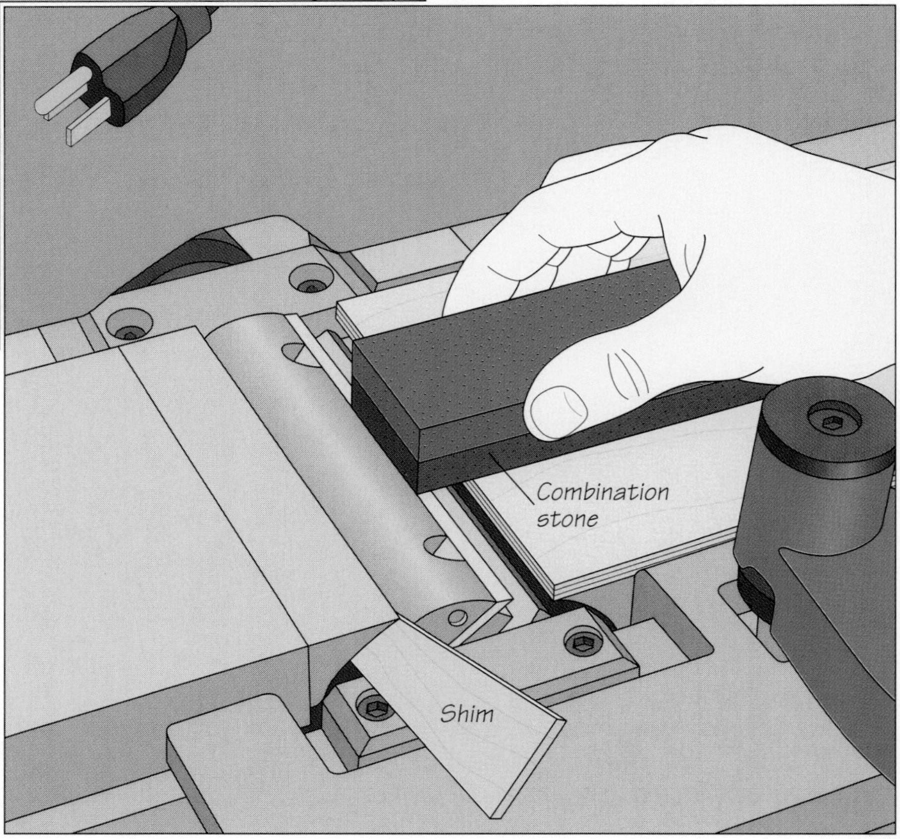

Knife
bevel

Combination
stone

Shim

3 Honing the knives

Slide a combination stone evenly across the beveled edge of the knife *(right)*. Move the stone with a side-to-side motion until the bevel is flat and sharp, avoiding contact with the cutterhead. Repeat the process to hone the remaining knives.

SHARPENING JOINTER KNIVES

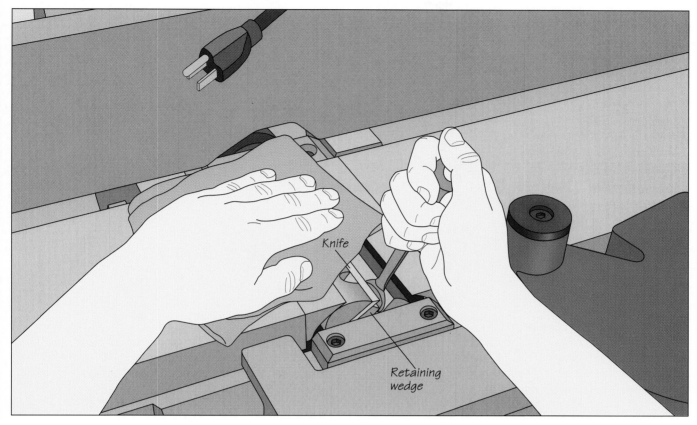

Knife

Retaining wedge

1 Removing the knives
To give jointer knives a full-fledged sharpening, remove them from the cutterhead. Unplug the machine, shift the fence away from the tables, and move the guard out of the way. Use a small wood scrap to rotate the cutterhead until the lock screws securing one of the knives are accessible between the tables. Cover the edge of the knife with a rag to protect your hands, then use a wrench to loosen each screw *(above)*. Lift the knife and the retaining wedge out of the cutterhead.

SHOP TIP

Shifting knives for longer life
To prolong the life of a set of jointer knives that have been nicked, loosen the lock screws securing one knife and slide the knife about ⅟₁₆ inch in either direction. Tighten the lock screws and carefully rotate the cutterhead by hand to ensure that the knife turns freely. Shifting a knife to one side moves its damaged segment out of alignment with the damage on the other knives, enabling the set to continue cutting smoothly.

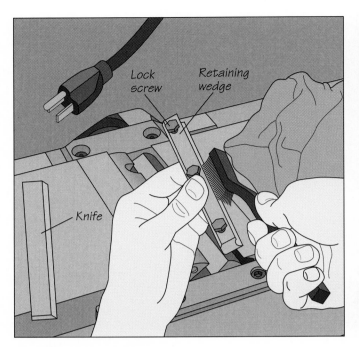

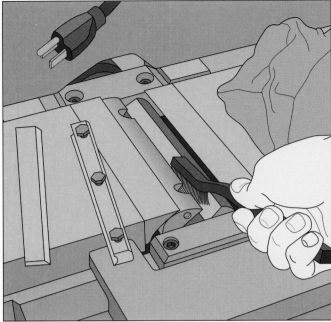

2 Cleaning the retaining wedge
Clean any pitch or gum from the retaining wedge using a brass-bristled brush dipped in solvent *(above, left)*. If the face of the retaining wedge that butts against the knife is pitted or rough, you may have trouble setting the knife height when rein-stalling the knife. Flatten the face of the wedge as you would the sole of a plane *(page 40)* until it is smooth. Also use the brush to clean the slot in the cutterhead that houses the retaining wedge and knife *(above, right)*.

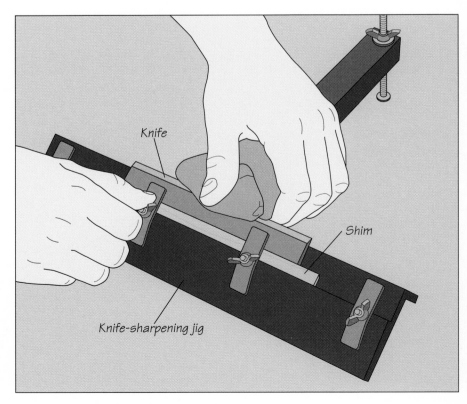

3 Installing the knife in a sharpening jig
Use a commercial knife-sharpening jig to sharpen the jointer knife. Center the knife in the jig bevel up and clamp it in place by tightening the wing nuts; use a rag to protect your hand *(right)*. Make sure that the blade is parallel with the lip of the jig. If the knife does not extend out far enough from the jig, insert a wood shim between the knife and the jig clamps.

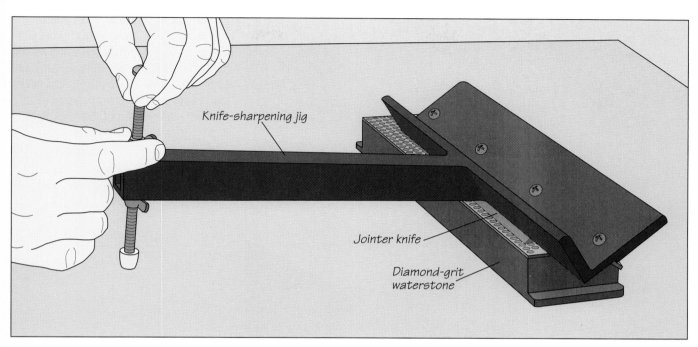

Knife-sharpening jig

Jointer knife

Diamond-grit
waterstone

4 Sharpening the knife

Set a sharpening stone on a flat, smooth work surface; in the illustrations on this page, a diamond-grit waterstone is shown. To adjust the jig so the beveled edge of the jointer knife is flat on the stone, turn the jig over, rest the bevel on the stone, and turn the wing nuts at the other end of the jig *(above)*. Lubricate the stone—in this case with water—and slide the knife back and forth. Holding the knob-end of the jig flat on the work surface and pressing the knife on the stone, move the jig in a figure-eight pattern *(below)*. Continue until the bevel is flat and sharp. Carefully remove the knife from the jig and hone the flat side of the knife to remove any burr formed in the sharpening process.

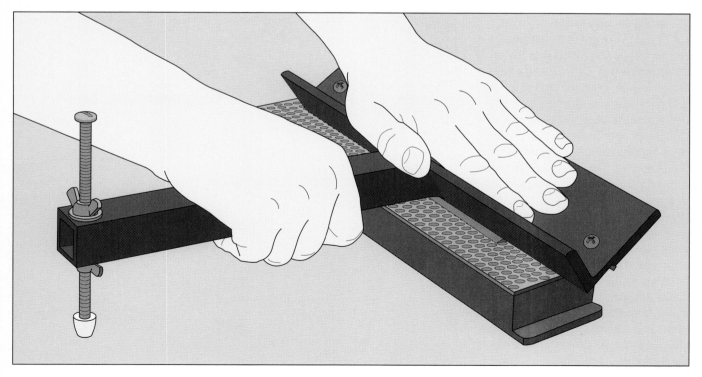

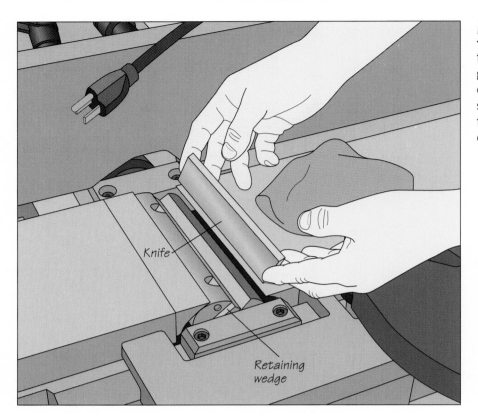

5 **Reinstalling the knife in the jointer**
Insert the retaining wedge in the cutterhead, centering it in the slot with its grooved edge facing up. With the beveled edge of the knife facing the outfeed table, slip it between the retaining wedge and the front edge of the slot, leaving the bevel protruding from the cutterhead.

6 **Setting the knife height**
Adjust the height of the knife using a commercial jig *(page 85)*, or do the job by hand, as shown at right. Cover the edge of the knife with a rag and partially tighten each lock screw on the retaining wedge. Use a small wooden wedge to rotate the cutterhead until the edge of the knife is at its highest point—also known as Top Dead Center or TDC. Then, holding the cutterhead stationary with a wedge, place a straight hardwood board on the outfeed table so that it extends over the cutterhead. The knife should just brush against the board along the knife's entire length. If not, use a hex wrench to adjust the knife jack screws. Once the knife is at the correct height, tighten the lock screws on the retaining wedge fully, beginning with the one in the center and working out toward the edges. Sharpen and install the remaining knives the same way.

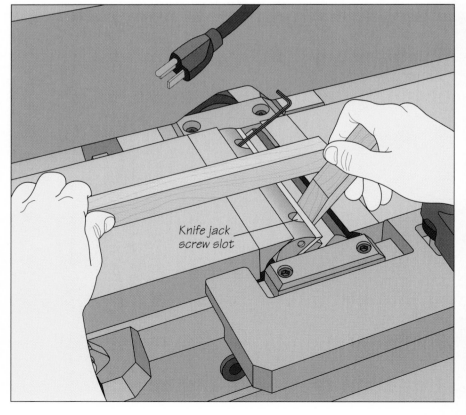

INSTALLING JOINTER KNIVES WITH A JIG

Using a knife-setting jig

The jig shown at right features magnetic arms that will hold a jointer knife at the correct height while you tighten the retaining wedge lock screws. Insert the knife in the cutterhead and position it at its highest point as you would to install the knife by hand *(page 84)*. Then mark a line on the fence directly above the cutting edge. Position the knife-setting jig on the outfeed table, aligning the reference line on the jig arm with the marked line on the fence, as shown. Mark another line on the fence directly above the second reference line on the jig arm. Remove the jig and extend this line across the outfeed table. (The line will help you quickly position the jig the next time you install a knife.) Reposition the jig on the table, aligning its reference lines with the marked lines on the fence. Then use a wrench to tighten the lock screws *(right)*.

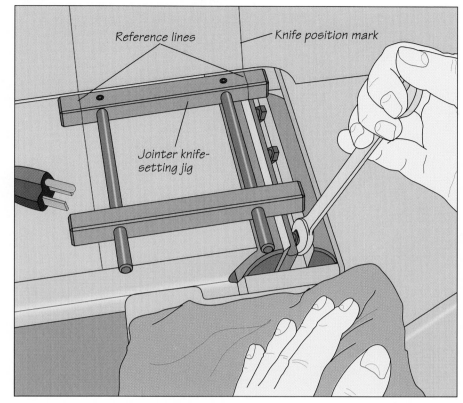

Reference lines

Knife position mark

Jointer knife-setting jig

SHARPENING PLANER KNIVES

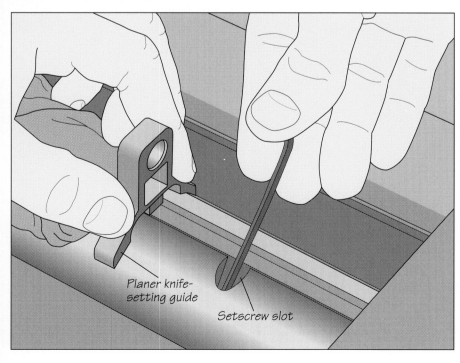

Planer knife-setting guide

Setscrew slot

Removing and installing a planer knife

Remove a planer knife from the machine and sharpen it as you would a jointer knife *(page 81)*. To reinstall the knife use the knife-setting guide supplied with the machine or a commercially available model like the one shown on page 79. Place the knife in the planer cutterhead and partially tighten the setscrews. Hold the knife-setting guide beside one of the setscrews so that its two feet are resting on the cutterhead on each side of the opening. Then adjust the setscrew with a hex wrench until the edge of the knife contacts the bottom of the guide *(left)*. Repeat for the remaining setscrews.

MAINTAINING PORTABLE POWER TOOLS

A belt sander in a commercial stand is paired with a plywood truing jig to correct a router's out-of-round sub-base, which can produce imprecise cuts. To correct the problem, install a centering pin in the router, drill a hole in the jig to hold the pin, and turn on the sander. Then slowly rotate the sub-base against the belt until it is perfectly round.

Whatever their price range or list of features, all portable power tools will work better and last longer if they are cared for properly. At its most basic, preventive maintenance is easy to do and takes no more than a few minutes. At the end of your work day, for example, get in the habit of cleaning dust and dirt from your tools. Refer to the schedules on page 88 for additional maintenance ideas. When you buy a new tool, register the warranty and file the owner's manual in a convenient place and follow all the operating and maintenance instructions suggested by the manufacturer. Owner's manuals typically include troubleshooting guides to help users recognize and handle malfunctions. Keep your tool's original packaging should you need to return an item for servicing.

Because portable tools are electrically powered, caring for them is as much a matter of safety as of performance. Today's power tools are designed to insulate the user from electrical shock, but any tool that develops an electrical problem can be hazardous. This chapter provides illustrations of the portable power tools commonly used in woodworking with cutaway views of their principal electrical and mechanical components. The drawings are designed to help show you where these parts are

typically located and recognize where a tool may have a problem.

Fortunately, the parts of a power tool that endure the most abuse and most often suffer damage are those that are also the easiest to access: the plugs, power cords, motor brushes, and on/off switches. As shown beginning on page 98, these components can be replaced easily and inexpensively. Before undertaking a repair, however, check whether the tool is still covered by the manufacturer's warranty. Opening up a tool that is still under warranty will usually void the guarantee.

The decision to repair other parts of a portable power tool, such as the motor and motor bearing, for example, depends on a number of factors, including your own abilities. Unless you feel comfortable making an electrical or mechanical repair, you are better off taking the tool to an authorized service center. If you do elect to open up a tool to repair or replace an internal component, label the wiring and the parts you disconnect to help you reassemble the tool properly. The age and value of a tool is also a consideration. The most worthwhile remedy for a 20-year-old drill with a burned-out motor may be a new drill rather than a new motor.

A combination square confirms that the blade of a circular saw is perpendicular to the tool's base plate. All power saws rely on this alignment for accurate cuts. To correct the adjustment, loosen the bevel adjustment knob shown in the photo at left and tilt the base plate until the square is flush against both the plate and blade, then tighten the knob.

MAINTENANCE TIPS AND SCHEDULES

There are no industry-wide standards for servicing portable power tools designed for the home shop. Manufacturers of industrial-use power tools issue maintenance schedules for their products, but these tools typically undergo heavier use than the average home workshop tool. For industrial tools, servicing is usually scheduled every 100 hours of use and includes a complete overhaul. Brushes are replaced, bearings are cleaned and lubricated (or replaced), and the wiring, motor, and other electrical components are checked and, if necessary, repaired.

For the typical power tool in the home shop, however, maintenance schedules and requirements are less clearcut. Much depends on how a tool is used. A circular saw used by the weekend woodworker to cut the occasional plank will obviously require less attention than one used by a busy carpenter or cabinetmaker who regularly relies on his tool to crosscut 8/4 stock and saw sheets of plywood to manageable lengths.

The chart below lists the checks that should be made on many portable power tools. The tasks listed are straightforward and can be done in a matter of minutes. How often you perform these checks will depend on your own needs and circumstances. As a rule of thumb, any tool that does not perform the way it is designed to should be investigated. You can do the work yourself, but be aware that troubleshooting electrical problems in a power tool requires specialized equipment as well as a sound knowledge of how to use it. If you are uncomfortable working with electricity, take the tool to an authorized service center for repair.

While tools made a few decades ago can be completely disassembled, many recent models feature internal components that are factory-sealed and virtually inaccessible. In some tools, for example, the bearings are mechanically pressed onto the motor spindle. Attempting to separate the bearing from the motor in such tools without the right instrument will destroy the bearing. Manufacturers claim that such developments in tool technology have produced more durable, longer-lasting products. While this is no doubt true, one consequence for the power tool buff of tools with no "user-serviceable parts" is that repairs can only be carried out by properly equipped service centers.

To get the most from your tools and keep repairs to a minimum, refer to the tips listed on the opposite page. Read your owner's manual before using a tool to make certain you can operate it properly. And never try to use a tool for a task for which it is not designed. A tool will fail when subjected to stress it is not built to handle.

Checking portable power tools
The chart at right lists the checks that should be made on portable power tools on a regular basis. Develop a timetable that suits your work habits. Tools that are used frequently or that get heavy use should be checked often.

TOOL	MAINTENANCE
Router	Check the collet for play and run out (page 91) Clean the collet and spindle Ensure that the sub-base is smooth and free of damage
Saber Saw	Check the guide rollers and blade supports for wear Check the blade clamp Check that base is square to blade
Plate Joiner	Check the plunge mechanism for play Check the blade and spindle for wear Inspect the pins and glides Inspect the drive belt
Electric Drill	Check the chuck bearing for play Inspect the chuck for wear
Belt Sander	Check the steel platen and cork pad for wear Check the drive belt Check the end roller for damage or excessive play Inspect the condition of the rubber on the drive roller
Circular Saw	Lubricate the gears Check the arbor bearings Check the guard return springs Check blade alignment
Orbital Sander	Check the pad for wear or splitting Check the eccentric bearing (on random-orbit sander) Check the pad support

MINIMUM WIRE GAUGE FOR EXTENSION CORDS

AMPERAGE RATING OF TOOL	MINIMUM GAUGE FOR DIFFERENT LENGTH CORDS		
	50'	75'	100'
0-2.0	18	18	18
2.1-3.4	18	18	16
3.5-5.0	18	16	14
5.1-7.0	16	14	12
7.1-12.0	14	12	10
12.1-16	12	10	8

Choosing the proper wire gauge

Using an extension cord with the wrong gauge may cause a drop in line voltage, resulting in a loss of power, excessive heat, and tool burnout. To determine the minimum wire gauge needed for the tool and task at hand, see the chart above. If, for instance, your tool has a 4-amp motor and you are using a 50-foot extension cord, the minimum gauge should be 18. Choose only round-jacketed extension cords listed by the Underwriters Laboratory (UL), or the Canadian Standards Association (CSA).

SHOP TIP

Storing bits

The cutting edges of router and drill bits, particularly those made of carbide, can be nicked if they are thrown together in storage. Protect your bits with a simple shop-made holder. In a block of wood, bore a series of holes the size of the bit shanks and store them with the cutting edge up.

MAINTENANCE TIPS FOR PORTABLE POWER TOOLS

• Read your owner's manual carefully before operating any tool.

• Do not use a tool if any of its parts is loose or damaged; inspect blades, bits, and accessories before starting an operation.

• Keep blades and bits clean and sharp; discard any that are chipped or damaged.

• Turn a tool off if it produces an unfamiliar vibration or noise; have the tool serviced before resuming operations.

• Do not leave a tool running when it is unattended.

• Follow the manufacturer's instructions to change blades, bits, or accessories; unplug the tool first.

• Before cutting, shaping, or sanding a workpiece, remove loose knots using a hammer; inspect salvaged wood for nails and screws before cutting.

• Do not attempt to cut through nails; this can cause kickback and also ruin a blade or bit.

• Use the appropriate wire gauge when replacing a damaged power cord or using an extension cord.

• Keep the power cord out of the tool's path; do not use the tool if the cord is frayed.

• Make sure the blade or bit is not in contact with the workpiece when you turn on a tool; allow the cutter to come to full speed before feeding it into the stock.

• Do not force a tool through a cut; this can snap a blade or cause it to veer off course. Allow the blade or bit to cut at its own speed.

• Make sure that any keys and adjusting wrenches are removed from the tool before turning it on.

• Keep a tool's air vents clear of sawdust to avoid overheating the motor.

• Do not use a tool for extended periods of time without allowing it to cool.

ANATOMY OF A ROUTER

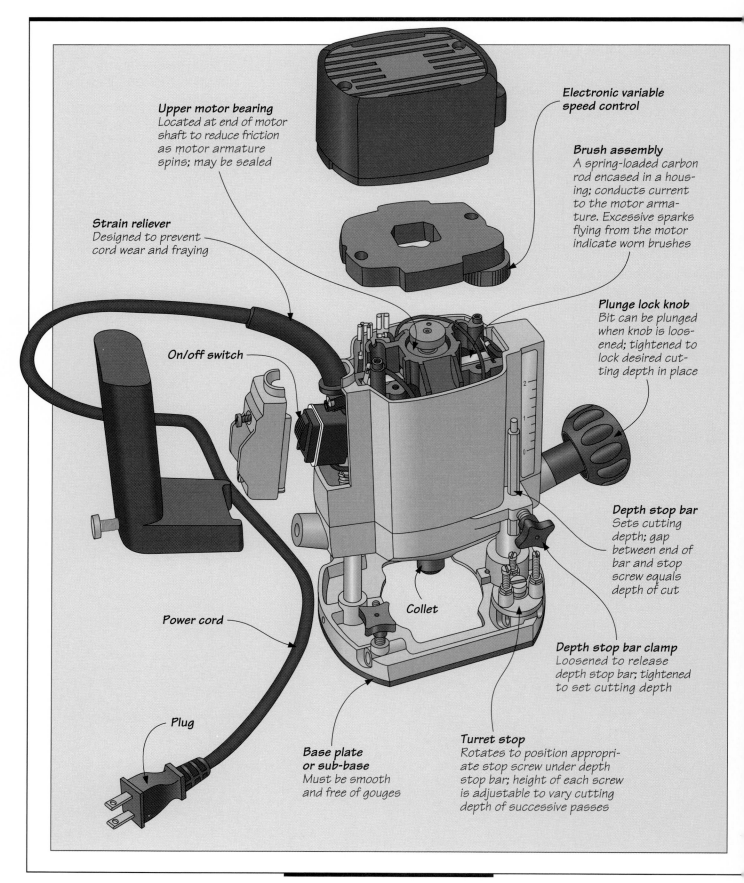

Upper motor bearing
Located at end of motor shaft to reduce friction as motor armature spins; may be sealed

Electronic variable speed control

Brush assembly
A spring-loaded carbon rod encased in a housing; conducts current to the motor armature. Excessive sparks flying from the motor indicate worn brushes

Strain reliever
Designed to prevent cord wear and fraying

On/off switch

Plunge lock knob
Bit can be plunged when knob is loosened; tightened to lock desired cutting depth in place

Depth stop bar
Sets cutting depth; gap between end of bar and stop screw equals depth of cut

Collet

Power cord

Depth stop bar clamp
Loosened to release depth stop bar; tightened to set cutting depth

Plug

Base plate or sub-base
Must be smooth and free of gouges

Turret stop
Rotates to position appropriate stop screw under depth stop bar; height of each screw is adjustable to vary cutting depth of successive passes

CHECKING THE COLLET FOR RUNOUT

Using a dial indicator and a magnetic base
Install a centering pin in the router as you would a bit and set the tool upside down on a metal surface, such as a table saw. Connect a dial indicator to a magnetic base and place the base next to the router. Turn on the magnet and position the router so the centering pin contacts the plunger of the dial indicator. Calibrate the dial indicator to zero following the manufacturer's instructions. Then turn the shaft of the router by hand to rotate the centering pin *(right)*. The dial indicator will register collet runout—the amount of wobble that the collet is causing the bit. If the runout exceeds 0.005 inch, replace the collet.

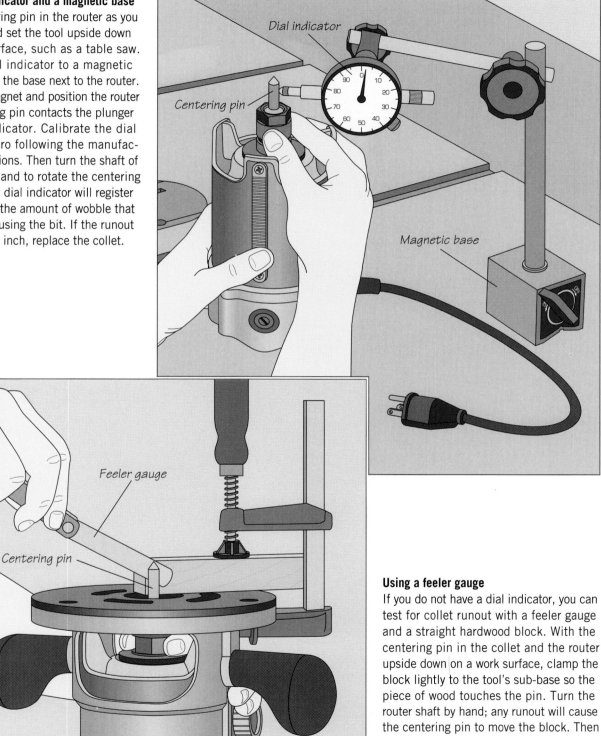

Dial indicator

Centering pin

Magnetic base

Feeler gauge

Centering pin

Using a feeler gauge
If you do not have a dial indicator, you can test for collet runout with a feeler gauge and a straight hardwood block. With the centering pin in the collet and the router upside down on a work surface, clamp the block lightly to the tool's sub-base so the piece of wood touches the pin. Turn the router shaft by hand; any runout will cause the centering pin to move the block. Then use a feeler gauge to measure any gap between the pin and the block *(left)*. If the gap exceeds 0.005 inch, replace the collet.

ANATOMY OF A SABER SAW

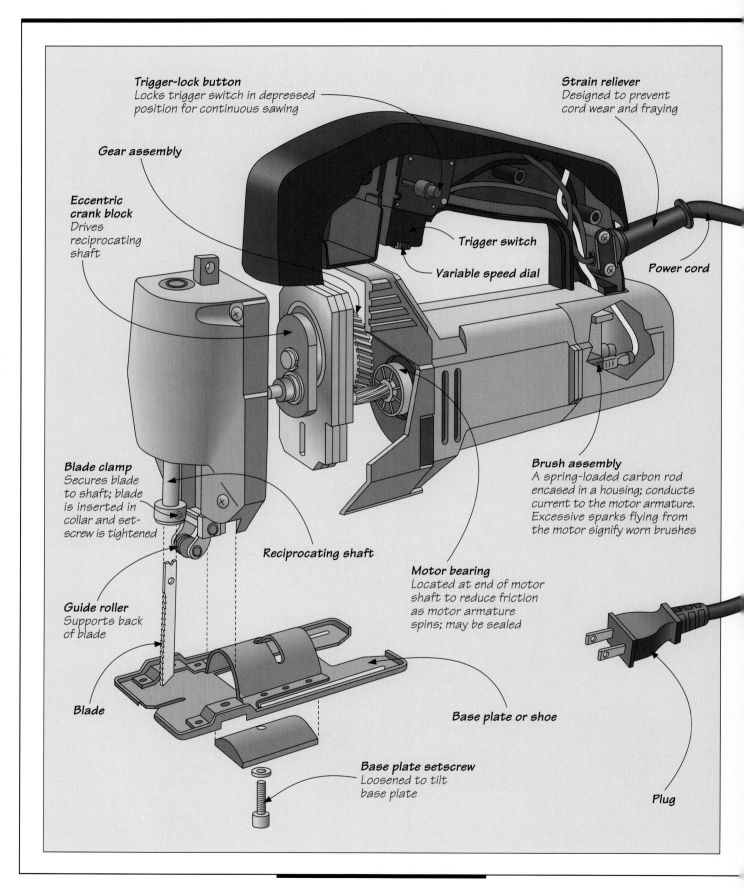

Trigger-lock button
Locks trigger switch in depressed position for continuous sawing

Gear assembly

Eccentric crank block
Drives reciprocating shaft

Strain reliever
Designed to prevent cord wear and fraying

Trigger switch

Variable speed dial

Power cord

Blade clamp
Secures blade to shaft; blade is inserted in collar and set-screw is tightened

Reciprocating shaft

Brush assembly
A spring-loaded carbon rod encased in a housing; conducts current to the motor armature. Excessive sparks flying from the motor signify worn brushes

Guide roller
Supports back of blade

Motor bearing
Located at end of motor shaft to reduce friction as motor armature spins; may be sealed

Blade

Base plate or shoe

Base plate setscrew
Loosened to tilt base plate

Plug

SQUARING THE BLADE

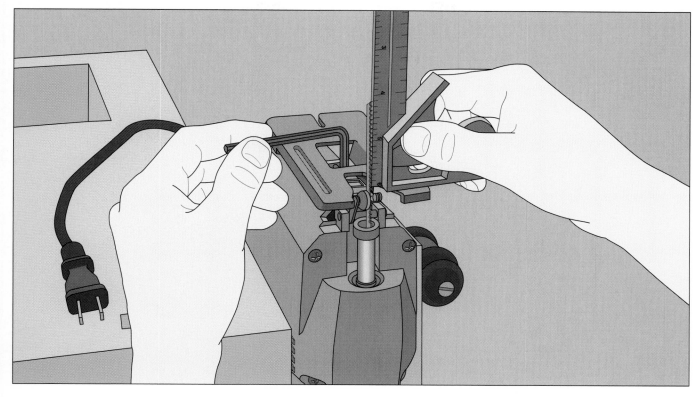

Checking the blade angle

Square a saber saw blade each time you install a new blade. Unplug the saw, then secure it upside down in a bench vise as shown above. Use a combination square to check whether the blade is square with the base plate. If not, loosen the base plate setscrew with a hex wrench and tilt the plate until the blade butts flush against the square. Then tighten the setscrew.

SHOP TIP

Extending blade life

If most of the stock you cut is ¾ inch or thinner, the top third of your blade will be the only portion showing wear. To make better use of the full length of the cutting edge, install an auxiliary shoe on the base plate of the saw once the top third of a blade begins to dull. To make the shoe, cut a piece of ½-inch plywood the same length as the base plate and slightly wider. Hold the wood against the plate and mark the outline of the notch cut out for the blade. Saw out the notch and cut a slot for the blade. Screw the auxiliary shoe in place, making sure that the back of the blade fits in the slot. (If the blade is not supported, it may wander and break when you are cutting.)

ANATOMY OF A PLATE JOINER

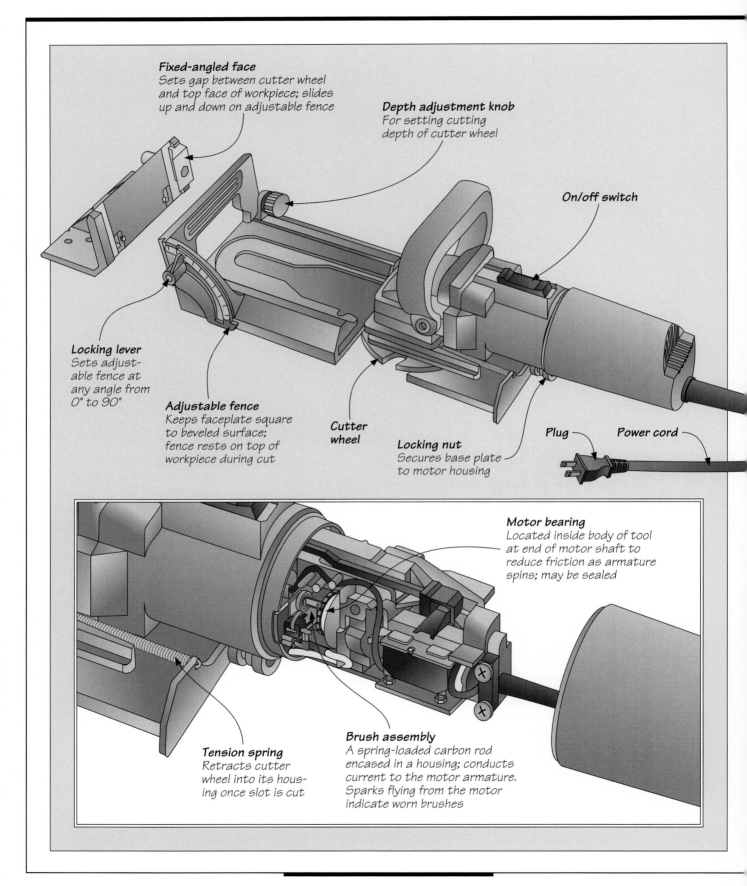

Fixed-angled face
Sets gap between cutter wheel
and top face of workpiece; slides
up and down on adjustable fence

Depth adjustment knob
For setting cutting
depth of cutter wheel

On/off switch

Locking lever
Sets adjust-
able fence at
any angle from
0° to 90°

Adjustable fence
Keeps faceplate square
to beveled surface;
fence rests on top of
workpiece during cut

**Cutter
wheel**

Locking nut
Secures base plate
to motor housing

Plug

Power cord

Motor bearing
Located inside body of tool
at end of motor shaft to
reduce friction as armature
spins; may be sealed

Tension spring
Retracts cutter
wheel into its hous-
ing once slot is cut

Brush assembly
A spring-loaded carbon rod
encased in a housing; conducts
current to the motor armature.
Sparks flying from the motor
indicate worn brushes

ANATOMY OF AN ELECTRIC DRILL

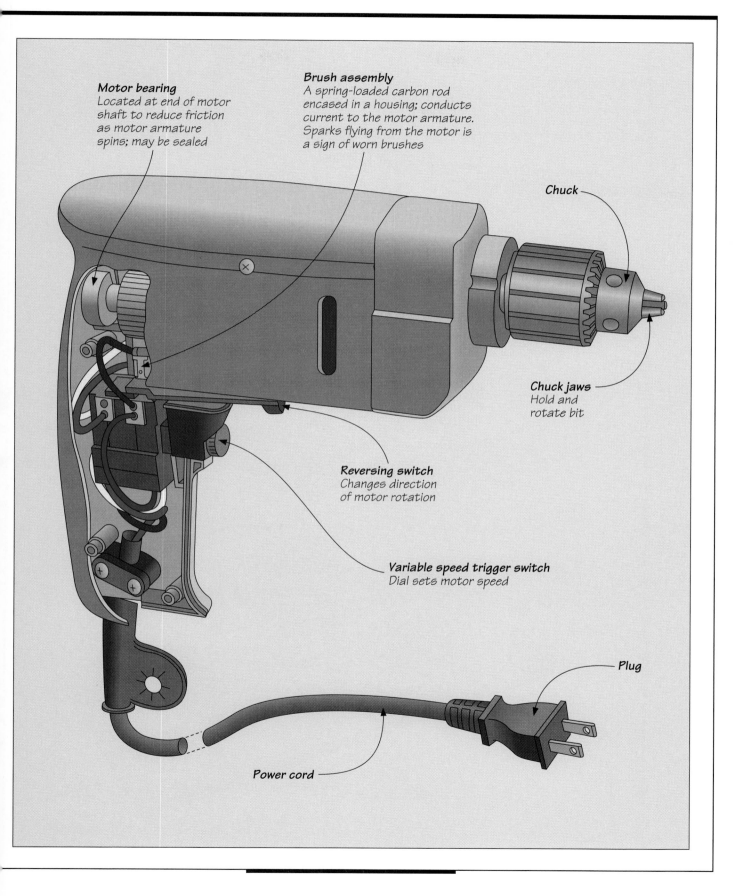

Motor bearing
Located at end of motor shaft to reduce friction as motor armature spins; may be sealed

Brush assembly
A spring-loaded carbon rod encased in a housing; conducts current to the motor armature. Sparks flying from the motor is a sign of worn brushes

Chuck

Chuck jaws
Hold and rotate bit

Reversing switch
Changes direction of motor rotation

Variable speed trigger switch
Dial sets motor speed

Plug

Power cord

ANATOMY OF A SANDER

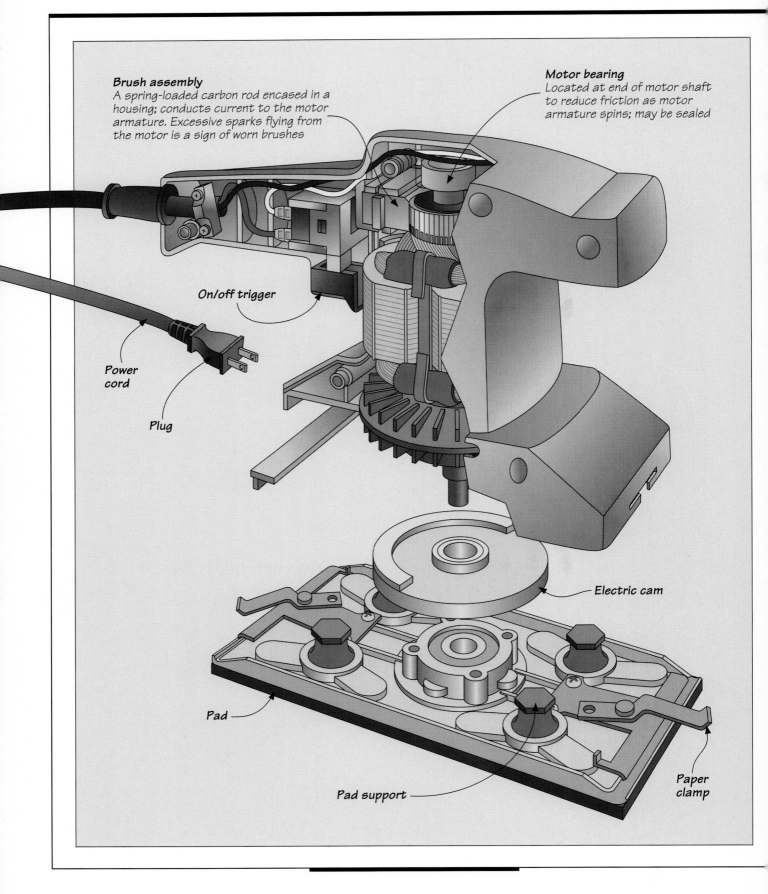

Brush assembly
A spring-loaded carbon rod encased in a housing; conducts current to the motor armature. Excessive sparks flying from the motor is a sign of worn brushes

Motor bearing
Located at end of motor shaft to reduce friction as motor armature spins; may be sealed

On/off trigger

Power cord

Plug

Electric cam

Pad

Pad support

Paper clamp

ANATOMY OF A CIRCULAR SAW

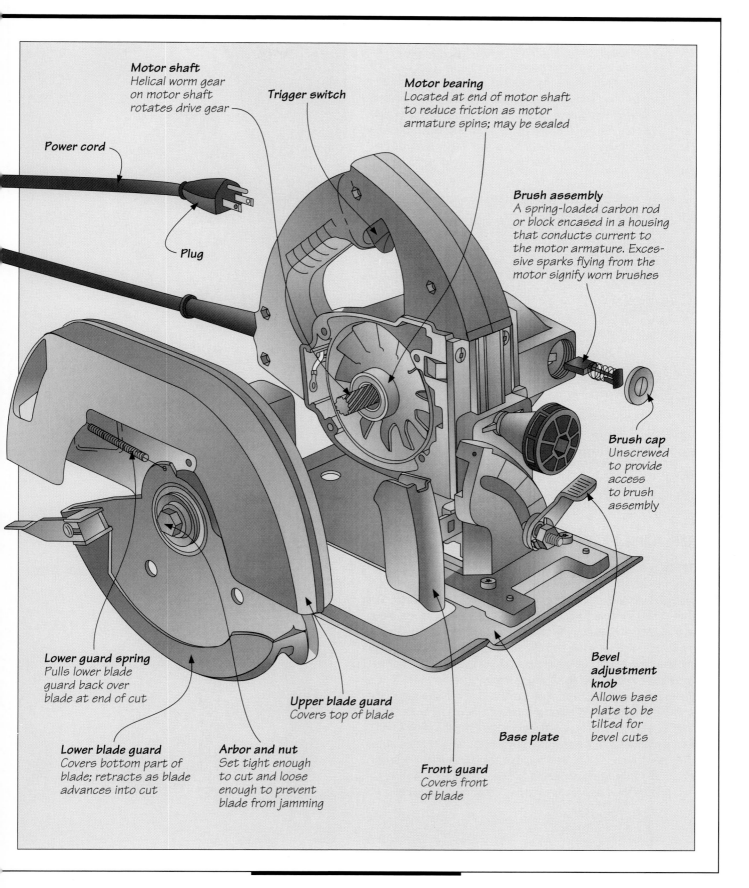

Motor shaft
Helical worm gear
on motor shaft
rotates drive gear

Trigger switch

Motor bearing
Located at end of motor shaft
to reduce friction as motor
armature spins; may be sealed

Power cord

Plug

Brush assembly
A spring-loaded carbon rod
or block encased in a housing
that conducts current to
the motor armature. Excessive sparks flying from the
motor signify worn brushes

Brush cap
Unscrewed
to provide
access
to brush
assembly

Lower guard spring
Pulls lower blade
guard back over
blade at end of cut

Upper blade guard
Covers top of blade

**Bevel
adjustment
knob**
Allows base
plate to be
tilted for
bevel cuts

Lower blade guard
Covers bottom part of
blade; retracts as blade
advances into cut

Arbor and nut
Set tight enough
to cut and loose
enough to prevent
blade from jamming

Front guard
Covers front
of blade

Base plate

The cap housing of a router is lifted off the body of the tool, revealing the wiring connections for the toggle switch inside. As shown in the photo at right, gaining access to the internal components of most portable power tools is simply a matter of loosening the retaining screws that secure the tool housing to the body. The cap providing access to the brush assembly for this router is located on the side of the tool body to the right of the switch.

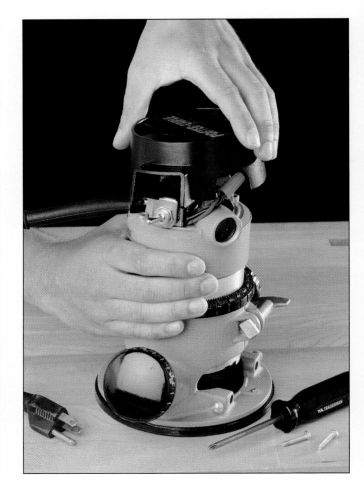

ELECTRICAL SAFETY TIPS

• Unplug a tool before undertaking any repair to its internal components; you may inadvertently contact current in a defective tool—even with the on/off switch turned off.

• Allow a power tool to cool before servicing it.

• Use only replacement parts that meet the same specifications as the originals.

• When a power tool stops working, determine whether or not the problem originates outside of it before you take it apart. Carefully examine the tool's power cord; a frayed cord or a broken plug is a common cause of failure.

• Before disassembling a power tool, make a diagram of wire connections to make reassembly easier.

• Before undertaking a repair, contact the manufacturer to find out if a service manual for the tool is available.

REPLACING A BRUSH ASSEMBLY

Removing and installing a brush assembly
Brushes are spring-loaded carbon rods or blocks that conduct electricity to the rotating armature of a power tool's motor. Over time, brushes wear or become damaged. You can access the assembly by unscrewing the brush cap on the tool body—normally a plastic cap roughly the size of a dime. If there is no brush cap, you will have to remove the motor housing to access the brushes. Once you have located the brush assembly, carefully lift it out of the tool. To test the brush, push on it to check the spring. If the spring is damaged or the brush is pitted, uneven, or worn shorter than its width, you will need to replace the assembly. Some brushes are marked with a wear line. Buy a replacement at an authorized service center for your brand of tool. To reinstall a brush assembly, fit it into position in the tool *(right)*. Then insert and tighten the brush cap or reattach the motor housing.

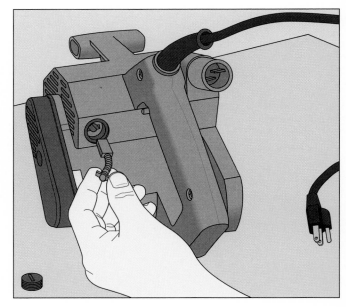

REPLACING A SWITCH

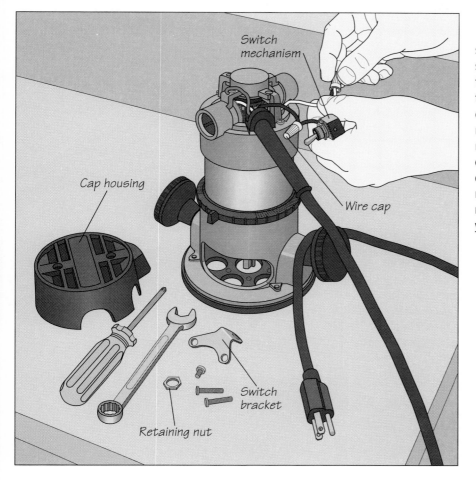

Switch
mechanism

Cap housing

Wire cap

Switch
bracket

Retaining nut

1 Removing the old switch
Set the tool on a work surface, making sure that it is unplugged. For the router shown at left, remove the cap housing to expose the switch mechanism. Loosen the switch retaining nut and screws, then disconnect the wires securing the mechanism to the tool. If the wires are connected by wire caps, simply loosen the caps *(left)* and untwist the wires. If the connections are soldered, snip the connections with pliers. Use short strips of masking tape to label the wires to help you reconnect them properly.

2 Installing the replacement switch
Buy a replacement switch at an authorized service center, noting the model and serial numbers of your tool. Connect the new switch to the wires in the tool housing, reversing the steps you took to take out the old one. Remove the masking tape strips from the wires, twist the wire ends from the tool and switch together, and screw a wire cap onto each connection to secure and insulate it. Fit the switch into position in the tool housing, screw the switch bracket in place, and tighten the switch retaining nut with a wrench *(right)*. Replace the tool's cap housing.

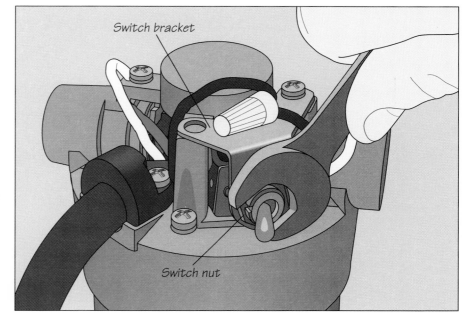

Switch bracket

Switch nut

REPLACING A POWER CORD

1 Accessing the cord's wire terminals
The wire terminals connecting a tool's power cord to the switch mechanism are contained within the motor housing. For the sander shown at right, reach the terminals by removing the auxiliary handle and loosening the screws securing the main handle to the tool body. Remove the handle to expose the wire terminals.

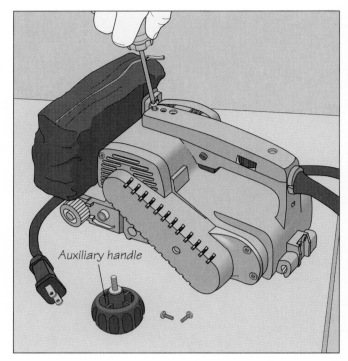

Auxiliary handle

2 Disconnecting the old power cord
On a power cord with a two-prong plug, there are usually two wires from the cord connected to wire terminal screws in the tool housing. Unscrew the plug retaining bracket securing the cord to the tool housing, loosen the terminal screws *(below)*, and carefully remove the power cord's wire ends from the terminals. Use strips of masking tape to label each terminal to help you attach the wire ends of the new cord to the appropriate terminals.

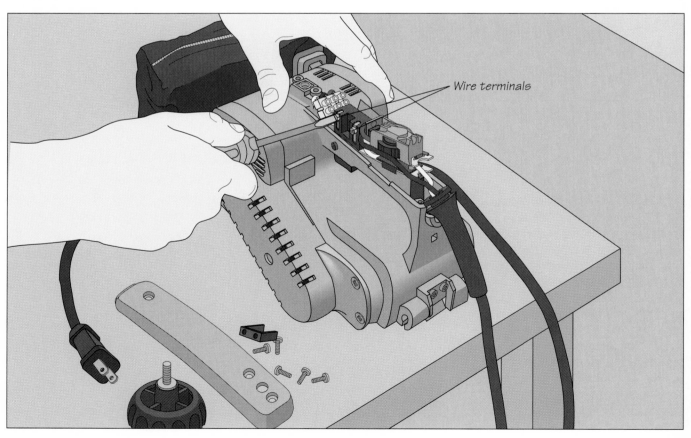

Wire terminals

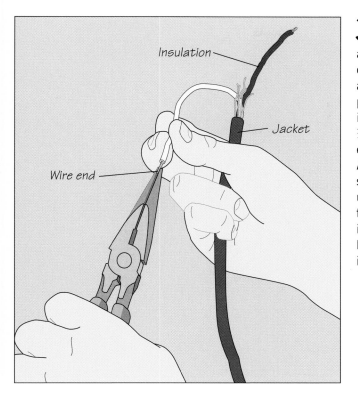

Insulation

Jacket

Wire end

3 Preparing the replacement power cord

Buy a replacement power cord at a hardware store or an authorized service center, making sure it has the same specifications as the original cord. The wire ends of new power cords are usually covered to the end with jacketing and insulation. To prepare the cord for installation, use a knife to cut away a few inches of the jacket covering the two wires. Then strip off about ½ inch of the plastic insulation around the wires, exposing the ends. You can also use wire strippers for this task *(page 102)*. Avoid cutting into the metal wire; if you sever any of the strands, snip off the damaged section and remove more insulation to uncover a fresh section. Use needle-nose pliers to carefully twist the wire strands snugly together *(left)*, then bend the wire ends into semicircles that will hug the terminals in the tool housing. Place the wire around the screw clockwise from the left side, so it will wrap around as the screw is tightened.

4 Installing the replacement cord

Hook the wire ends around the terminals in the tool housing, making sure to attach each wire to the appropriate screw. Remove the masking tape. Holding the power cord in position, screw the cord retaining bracket in place *(below)*, then reinstall the handles on the tool body.

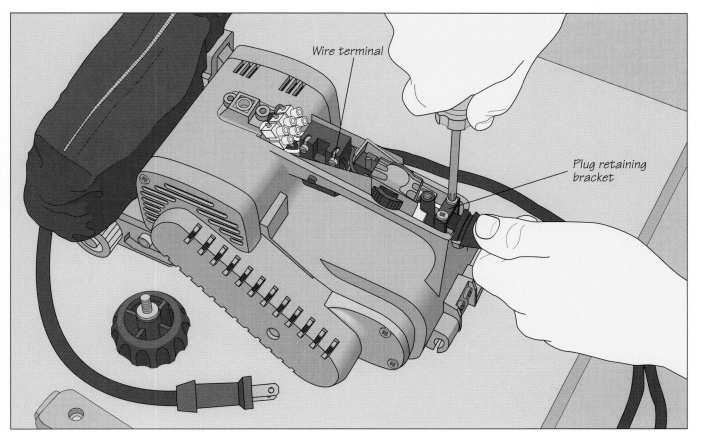

Wire terminal

Plug retaining bracket

REPLACING A PLUG

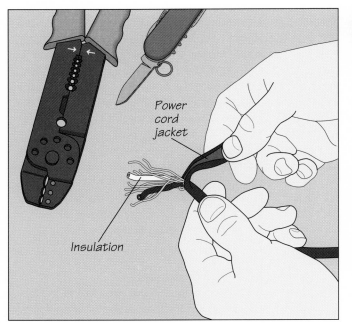

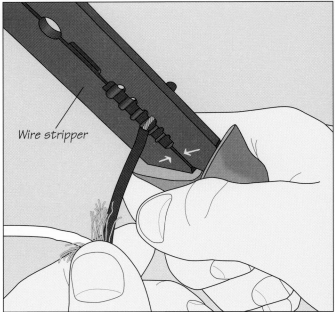

1 Removing the old plug and preparing the power cord
Use a knife to slice through the power cord just above the plug. Prepare the cut end of the power cord for the replacement plug as you would when replacing a new power cord *(page 100)*. Start by cutting away about 2 inches of the cord jacket with a knife *(above, left)*, then removing about ½ inch of insulation to expose the bare wire. This can be done with the knife or wire strippers. With the strippers, simply insert the wire end into the appropriate-size opening, squeeze the jaws of the strippers together *(above, right)*, and pull the wire out. The device will sever the insulation. Then use needle-nose pliers to twist the wire ends together and form them into a hook.

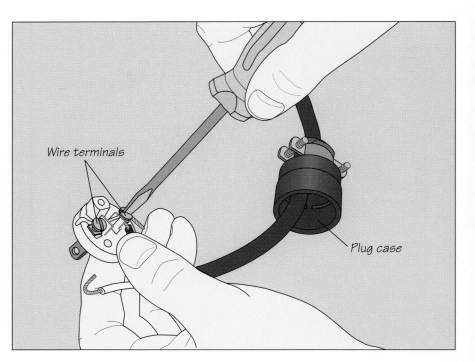

2 Connecting the power cord to the replacement plug
Buy a plug at a hardware store, making sure it has the same number and shape of prongs as the original. The plug shown consists of two parts: the prong section, which includes the terminal, a plug case, and retaining screws that hold the two parts together. Slip the end of the power cord through the plug case, then attach each wire end to the terminals on the plug *(right)*, tightening the screws to hold the wire ends securely.

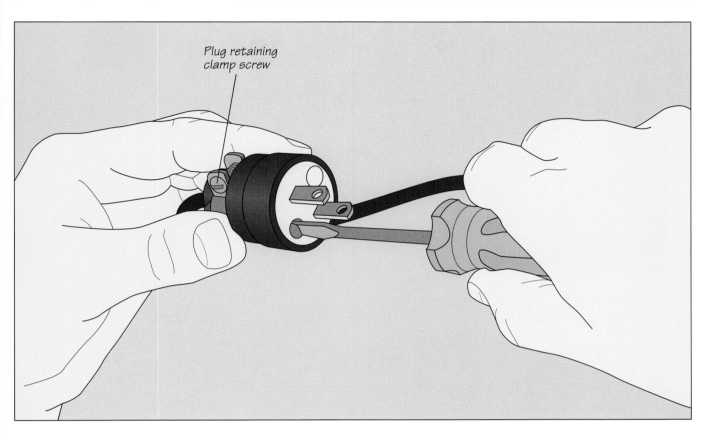

Plug retaining
clamp screw

3 Assembling the plug
Once the power cord wires are connected to the plug, assemble the two parts of the plug. Pull the casing over the plug and tighten the retaining screws until they are snug *(above)*. To complete the repair, tighten the plug retaining clamp screw. This will securely hold the plug and the power cord together.

SHOP TIP

Disabling a power tool
To prevent unauthorized use of a power tool, slip the bolt of a mini-padlock through one of the tines in the power cord plug. The lock will make it impossible to plug in the tool. If you are using a keyed lock, store the keys out of the way in a cupboard or drawer that can be locked.

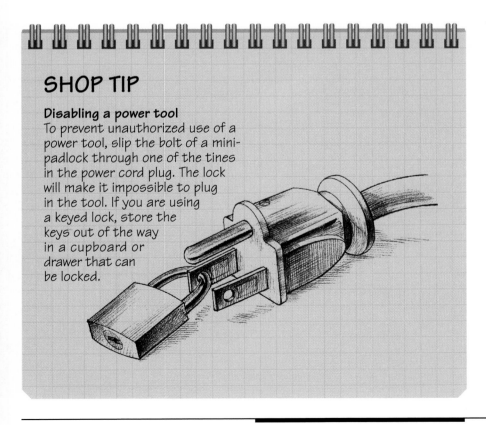

MAINTAINING STATIONARY POWER TOOLS

The precision and consistency we expect from stationary woodworking machines are only possible if the equipment is kept clean and finely tuned. Whether you have a cantankerous old band saw that needs to be cajoled into making a straight cut, or a brand-new radial arm saw that has slipped out of alignment on the way from the factory, learning how to adjust your stationary machines properly will improve the results and increase your pleasure from them.

Many woodworkers are apprehensive about exploring the nuts and bolts of their tools, and many owner's manuals do not encourage tinkering. However, most stationary power tools are quite simple in their design and construction. Taking the top off a table saw, which sounds like a major operation, is fairly simple to do and it can quickly reveal how the machine works, and exactly what you should clean, adjust, or tweak to keep it running smoothly.

The chapter that follows presents the major stationary power tools used by woodworkers and explains the basic maintenance and troubleshooting procedures for each one. Some of

A magnetic-base dial indicator checks the spindle of a drill press for runout—the amount of wobble that the spindle would transmit to a bit or accessory. For accurate drilling, the runout should not exceed 0.005 inch. If it does, the spindle should be replaced or repaired (see page 131).

these tasks, such as checking belts, cleaning switches, and keeping tabletops clean *(page 106)*, apply to most of the tools. Other maintenance tasks are specific to the design of a particular machine, such as cleaning and adjusting the blade height and tilt mechanisms on a table saw *(page 112)*, fixing an unbalanced band saw wheel *(page 122)*, or bleeding water from an air compressor *(page 139)*.

Knowing how to tune up your stationary tools will not only give you a deeper understanding of how they work; it will also provide you with a list of things to check when shopping for used models. Is a jointer's fence square? How much runout does a drill press chuck have? Does the miter gauge of a table saw slide smoothly?

Many woodworkers tune up their stationary tools just before the start of a major project. This can be difficult to schedule if you are one of those woodworkers who has many projects on the go. In such cases, it is a good idea to devote a little time periodically to maintaining your stationary tools. That way, every project will benefit from the best your tools can give.

With the wheel covers open, a long straightedge confirms that the wheels of a band saw are parallel to each other and in the same vertical plane. As shown in the photo at left, the straightedge should rest flush against the top and bottom of each wheel. The tilt knob on the top wheel can be adjusted to bring the top wheel into proper alignment.

Drive belts transmit power from the motor to the moving parts in many stationary power tools, including the jointer, disc sander, planer, and table saw. In high-torque tools such as the table saw shown in the photo at right, three belts are used to drive the arbor. Any drive belt that is cracked or worn extensively should be replaced.

CHECKING DRIVE BELTS

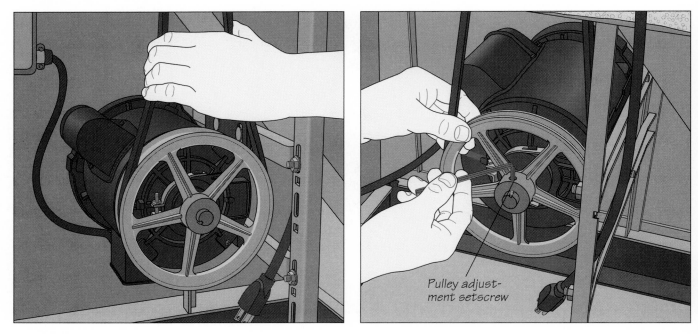

Pulley adjust-ment setscrew

Checking belt tension

Too much belt tension can strain a stationary tool's motor bearings, while too little tension often leads to slippage and excessive wear. To check drive belt tension on the jointer shown above, unplug the tool and remove the panel covering the belt. Then pinch the belt between the pulleys with one hand *(above, left)*. The amount of deflection will vary with the tool; as a rule of thumb, the belt should flex $\frac{1}{32}$ inch for every inch of span between pulleys. If there is too little or too much tension, adjust it following the manufacturer's instructions. For smooth operation, the pulleys should be aligned; if they are not, loosen the adjustment setscrew on the motor pulley with a hex wrench *(above, right)*, and slide the pulley in line with the other pulley.

MAINTAINING TABLETOPS

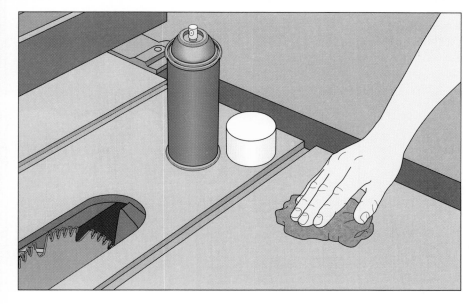

Cleaning a stationary machine tabletop
To keep stock running smoothly, clean the tabletop frequently, wiping off any pitch or gum deposits with a rag and mineral spirits. Remove any rust or pitting with fine steel wool and penetrating oil *(left)*, then wipe off any residue and sand the area with fine sandpaper. A coat of paste wax rubbed on and then buffed will make pushing wood into the cutting edge much less tiring.

MAINTAINING SWITCHES

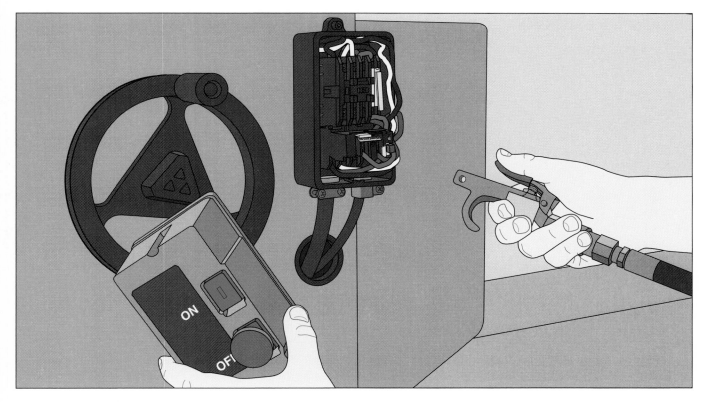

Cleaning a power switch
The switches on stationary tools can become clogged, causing the switch to stick or even preventing it from operating. If the switch sticks, unplug the tool, remove the switch cover and clean the switch immediately. To prevent such problems, periodically clean out the switch by blowing compressed air into it *(above)*.

TABLE SAWS

The table saw is the cornerstone of many workshops, put to use in nearly every phase of every project. Because of its crucial role, your table saw must be consistently accurate and its parts square and true. The normal forces of routine use will eventually throw a table saw out of alignment. Even a new machine straight off the assembly line usually needs a certain amount of adjustment before it can perform safely and properly.

The table saw components that need to be checked and aligned are those that come in contact with the workpiece during the cut: the blade, table, miter gauge, and rip fence. If any of these parts is not in proper alignment, you risk burn marks, tapered cuts, or kickback.

The simple tune-up procedures shown below and on the pages that follow will improve the performance of any table saw. It is a good idea to take the time to undertake them before starting a new project. For the sake of efficiency, follow the steps in the order they appear. You will only be able to align the miter gauge with the saw blade, for example, if the table has been squared with the blade. For safety, remember to unplug your saw before performing these checks and adjustments.

Most table saws feature worm gear and rack mechanisms connected to crank wheels to raise and tilt the arbor assembly and blade. These mechanisms can become caked with pitch and sawdust, preventing the saw from operating smoothly. In the photo at right, compressed air is being used to clean the blade height mechanism.

CHECKING TABLE ALIGNMENT

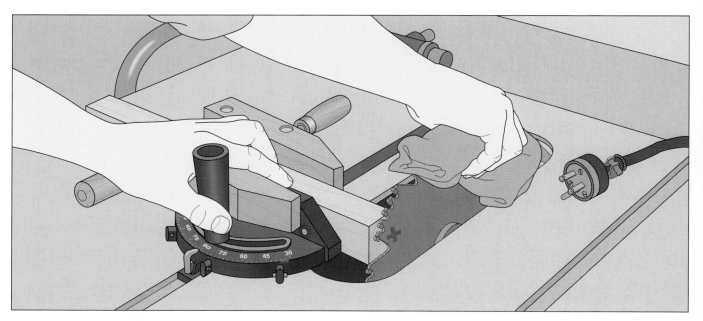

1 Checking the table alignment
The face of the miter gauge and the blade must be perfectly perpendicular. To check this, position the miter gauge at the front of the saw blade. Clamp a square wood block against the miter gauge with the end of the block butted against a saw blade tooth. Mark an X on the blade next to the tooth; this will enable you to check the same section of blade should you need to repeat the test after performing step 2. Slide the miter gauge and the block together toward the back of the table while rotating the blade by hand *(above)*. The block should remain butted against the tooth as the blade rotates from front to back. If a gap opens between the block and the tooth, or the block binds against the blade as it is rotated, you will need to align the table *(step 2)*.

2 Aligning the saw table

Adjust the saw table following the owner's manual instructions. For the model shown, use a hex wrench to loosen the table bolts that secure the top to the saw stand *(right)*; the bolts are located under the table. Loosen all but one of the bolts and adjust the table position slightly; the bolt you leave tightened will act as a pivot, simplifying the alignment process. Repeat the blade test *(step 1)*. Once the table is correctly aligned with the blade, tighten the table bolts.

3 Checking the blade angle

Remove the table insert, then butt a combination square against the saw blade between two teeth *(left)*. The blade of the square should fit flush against the saw blade. If there is a gap between the two, rotate the blade angle adjustment crank until the saw blade rests flush against the square's blade. Reposition the angle adjustment stop so that the blade will return to its proper position each time it is adjusted.

SQUARING THE MITER GAUGE

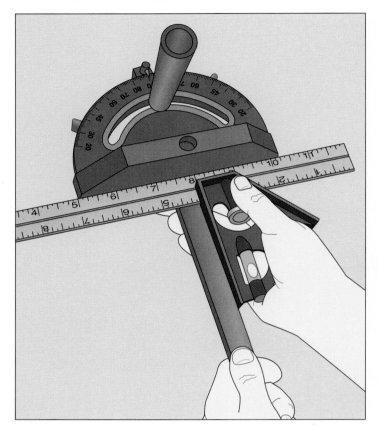
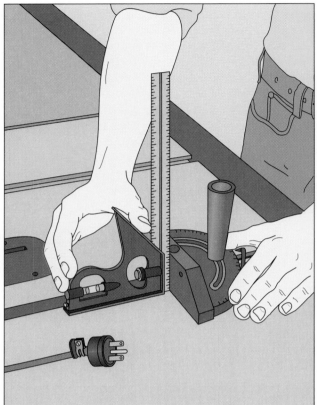

Aligning the miter gauge with the saw table
With the miter gauge out of the table slot, use a combination square to confirm that the face of the gauge is square with the edge of the gauge bar *(above, left)*. If it is not, use the adjustment handle on the gauge to square the two. Then place the miter gauge in its table slot and butt the square against the gauge *(above, right)*. The blade of the square should fit flush against the gauge. If there is a gap between the two, have the gauge machined square at a metal-working shop.

SHOP TIP

Fixing a loose miter gauge
To eliminate excessive side-to-side play of the miter gauge in its slot, remove the gauge from the table and place the bar edge up on a board. Use a ball-peen hammer and a prick punch to strike the edge of the bar in a staggered pattern every inch along it. This will raise bumps on the edge of the bar and result in a tighter fit in the slot. If the fit is too tight, file the bumps down as necessary.

TESTING THE TABLE SAW FOR SQUARE

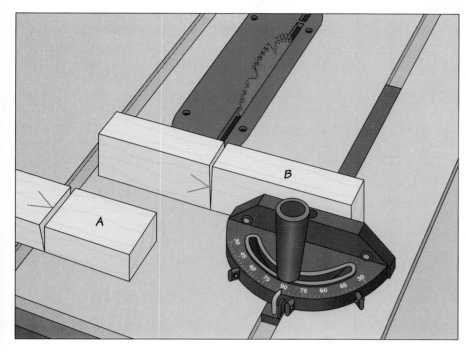

Checking your adjustments

Test the accuracy of your table saw adjustments by crosscutting a couple of scrap boards. To check the blade-to-table alignment, mark an X on a board and cut it face down at your mark. Then turn the cutoff over and hold the cut ends together *(board A in the illustration at left)*. Any gap between the two ends represents twice the error in the table alignment; if necessary, repeat the test shown in step 3 on page 109. To check the miter gauge adjustment, crosscut the second board, face down as well, flip one piece over, and butt the two pieces together on edge *(board B)*. Again, any gap represents twice the error in the adjustment. If necessary, square the miter gauge again *(page 110)*.

ALIGNING THE RIP FENCE

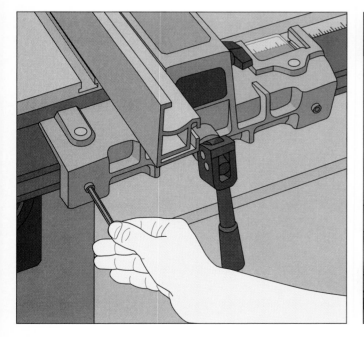

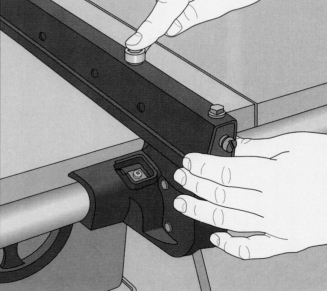

Adjusting the rip fence

Lock the rip fence in place alongside the miter slot. If the fence and the slot are not parallel, adjust the angle of the fence following the manufacturer's instructions. Some models feature adjustment bolts at the front of the table that you can loosen or tighten with a hex wrench to change the alignment *(above, left)*; others have fence adjustment bolts that you can loosen with a wrench *(above, right)*. For this model, adjust the fence parallel to the miter slot, then retighten the adjustment bolts.

LEVELING THE TABLE INSERT

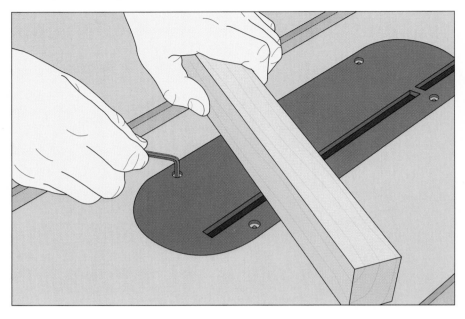

Adjusting the leveling screws
To set the table insert level with the saw table, place a square board across the insert and the table. Adjust the leveling screws at the corners of the insert with a hex wrench *(left)* until the insert is flush with the tabletop. You can also adjust the insert slightly below the table at the front and slightly above the table at the back; this will prevent the workpiece from catching or binding on the insert during the cut. If your saw's insert does not have leveling screws, file or shim the insert to make it lie flush with the table.

ADJUSTING THE HEIGHT AND TILT MECHANISMS

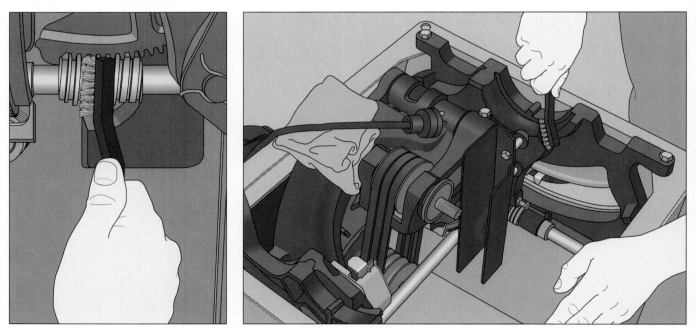

Cleaning the trunnions
If your table saw's blade sticks or moves sluggishly when you raise or tilt it, clean the height and tilt adjustment mechanisms inside the saw. Start by removing the tabletop following the manufacturer's instructions. Blow out the sawdust with compressed air, then clean the moving parts within the saw. Start with the blade height and tilt mechanisms *(above, left)*, using solvent and a brass-bristle brush to remove stubborn pitch and hardened sawdust deposits. Then scrub the machined ways on the front and rear trunnions *(above, right)*. Once all the parts are clean, lubricate all the moving parts with a graphite or silicon-based lubricant; oil and grease should be avoided as they tend to collect dust. Replace the tabletop and fine-tune the saw *(page 108)*.

RADIAL ARM SAWS

A radial arm saw's many pivoting and sliding parts enable you to pull a blade through a workpiece in a variety of angles and directions. This flexibility, however, can lead to problems. Unless the saw's moving parts are kept in alignment, its performance can become sloppy and potentially dangerous.

The procedures that follow will help you fine-tune a radial arm saw so that it will cut accurately and safely. Adjusting a radial arm saw can be time-consuming because of its many moving parts. To make the adjustments manageable, you can perform them in two steps: testing and adjusting the table, clamps and roller bearings *(page 114)*, and aligning and squaring the blade *(page 117)*.

For safety, unplug your saw while performing these checks and adjustments.

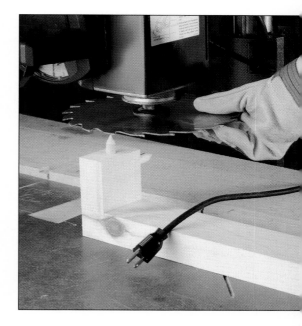

One of the most common problems with the radial arm saw is blade rotation that is not parallel or perpendicular to the table, known as blade heel. A simple L-shaped sounding jig shown in the photo at right can help you diagnose and correct heeling. A blade that is turning true will produce a uniform sound as its teeth brush against the sharpened dowel projecting from the jig. The sound of a heeling blade will change as its teeth touch the dowel.

CLEANING THE SLIDING MECHANISMS

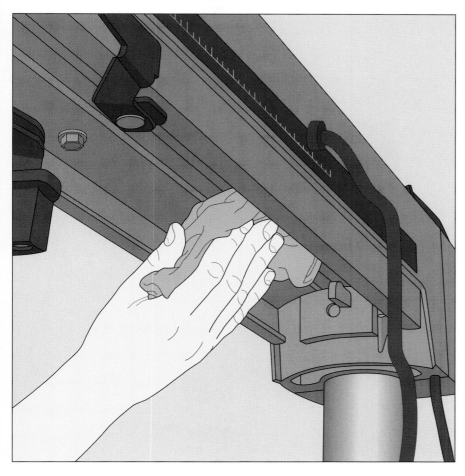

Cleaning the track and bearings
Use a solution of ammonia and water to clean your radial arm saw's track and roller bearings. Pull the yoke as far back as it will go, then wipe the track using a clean rag dampened with the solvent *(left)*. Push the yoke toward the column and clean the front portion of the track. Next, clean the roller bearings, located to the front and rear of the carriage that connects the yoke to the arm. Wrap the rag around your finger, dip it in the solvent, and hold it against the roller bearing while pushing the yoke away from you. Coat the track and bearings with light machine oil, then wipe off the excess.

ADJUSTING THE TABLE

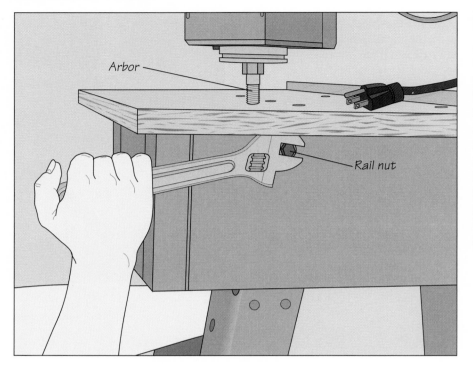

Leveling the table with the arm
Tilt the saw's motor until the arbor points down, its end slightly above table level. Then swivel the arm to position the arbor over the rail nuts on both sides of the table; in each position measure the gap between the arbor and the table. If the measurements are not equal, raise the low end of the table by turning the rail nut in a clockwise direction, using the head of an adjustable wrench to lever up the table surface *(left)*. Then make the same adjustment on the other side of the table. Repeat the measurements to make sure the table is level.

ADJUSTING THE CLAMPS

1 Adjusting the miter clamp
Swivel the arm to the right to a position between 0° and 45°. Lock the miter clamp, which on the saw shown is located at the front end of the arm. Try to push the end of the arm toward the 0° position *(right)*. If there is any play in the arm, adjust the clamp that holds it in place. For the model shown, use a hex wrench to tighten the miter clamp adjustment screw, located inside an access hole at the back end of the arm.

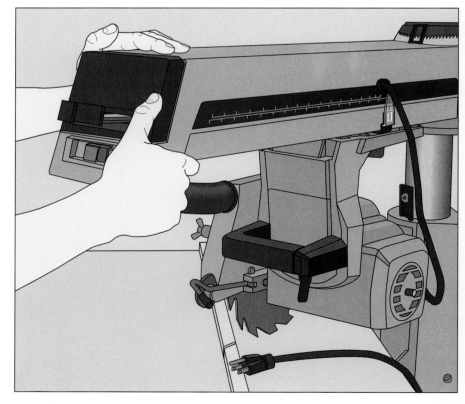

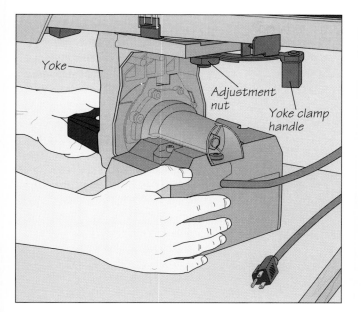

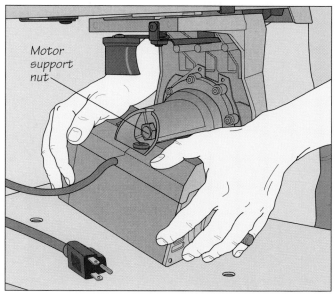

2 Adjusting the yoke clamp
Rotate the yoke to a position between the ones used for crosscutting and ripping. Lock the yoke clamp handle, then use both hands to try and push the motor to the crosscutting position *(above)*. The motor should not budge; if it does, adjust the clamp that locks it in position. For the model shown, tighten the adjustment nut located under the arm following the manufacturer's instructions. Lock the clamp and check again for play.

3 Adjusting the bevel clamp
Tilt the motor to a position between 0° and 45°. Lock the bevel clamp, then use both hands to try to move the motor *(above)*. If there is any looseness, adjust the clamp. For the model shown, use a socket wrench to tighten the motor support nut at the back of the motor, then release the clamp and try tilting the motor to each of the preset angles; if you cannot move the motor, loosen the support nut slightly. Otherwise, lock the clamp again and check once more for play in the motor.

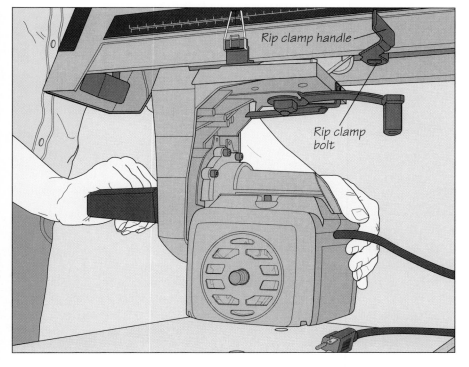

4 Adjusting the rip clamp
Lock the rip clamp, then use both hands to try to slide the yoke along the arm *(left)*. The yoke should not move; if it does, adjust the clamp. For the model shown, release the clamp, then use a wrench to tighten the nut at the end of the rip clamp bolt. Try sliding the yoke along the arm; if it binds, loosen the lock nut slightly. Otherwise, recheck the clamp and tighten the nut further if needed.

CARING FOR THE SLIDING MECHANISMS

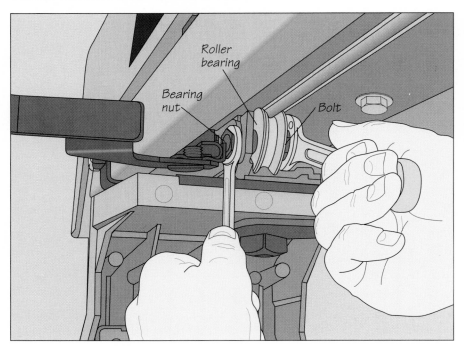

Roller bearing

Bearing nut

Bolt

1 Adjusting the carriage roller bearings
To check the carriage roller bearings, press your thumb against each one in turn while sliding the carriage away from your hand. The bearings should turn as the carriage slides along the arm. If your thumb keeps one of them from turning, you will need to tighten the bearing; if the carriage binds on the arm, a bearing will need to be loosened. In either case, adjust the bearing while holding the bolt stationary with a second wrench *(left)*. Tighten or loosen the bolt as required, then retighten the nut.

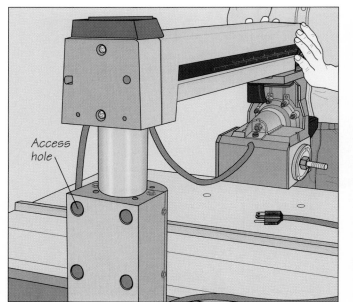

Access hole

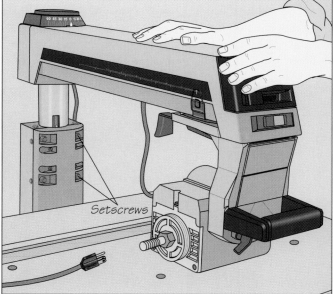

Setscrews

2 Adjusting column-to-base tension
Wipe the column clean, then loosen the four setscrews on the front of the column base using a hex wrench. To check column-to-base tension, use both hands to try to lift the end of the arm *(above, left)*; there should be little or no give to the column. Turn the elevating crank in both directions; the arm should slide smoothly up and down. If there is excessive movement at the column-to-base joint, or if the arm jumps or vibrates as it is raised or lowered, adjust the four bolts located in the access holes on the back cover of the base. Repeat the tests and, if necessary, make additional adjustments. Then try pushing the arm sideways *(above, right)*; if there is any rotation of the column, tighten the setscrews just enough to prevent movement. Run through the tests a final time, fine-tuning the adjustments.

SQUARING THE BLADE

1 Squaring the blade with the table
Set the saw's yoke in the crosscutting position and install a blade. Release the bevel clamp and tilt the motor counterclockwise as far as it will go in the 0° position. Relock the clamp. To check the blade position, butt a framing square between two saw teeth *(right)*. The square should fit flush against the side of the blade. If any gap shows between them, adjust the bevel clamp setscrews and tilt the motor to bring the blade flush against the square.

Bevel clamp setscrews

2 Squaring the blade with the fence
Release the miter clamp and swivel the arm to the right as far as it will go in the 0° position, then relock the clamp. Release the rip clamp and butt one arm of a framing square against the fence while the other just touches the blade tooth nearest to the table. Holding the blade steady, slide the yoke along the arm *(left)*; pull slowly to avoid dulling the tooth. The blade should make a constant rubbing sound as it moves along the edge of the square. If a gap opens up between the blade and the square, or if the blade binds, adjust the setscrews in the column base following the manufacturer's instructions.

CORRECTING BLADE HEEL

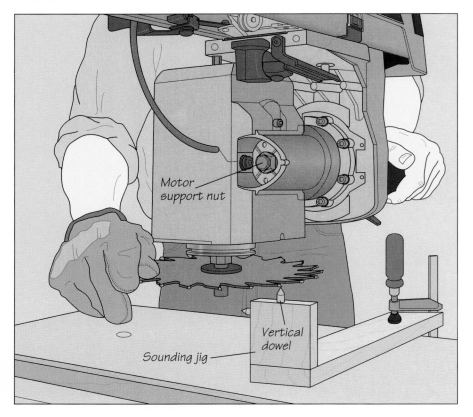

Motor support nut

Vertical dowel

Sounding jig

1 Fine-tuning horizontal rotation
Install a blade and set the motor in its horizontal position; tilt the motor counterclockwise as far as it will go, then lock the bevel clamp. To test for blade heel, build an L-shaped sounding jig and bore two holes in it. Sharpen the ends of two dowels and fit them into the jig as shown. Then position the jig to align a blade tooth near the back of the table directly over the vertical dowel. Lower the blade until the tooth rests lightly on the dowel; clamp the jig in place. Wearing a work glove, spin the blade backward, listen, and carefully note the sound *(left)*. Slide the yoke along the arm to align a tooth near the front of the table over the dowel and repeat the test. The sound should be the same in both positions. If it is not, adjust the motor support nut according to the manufacturer's instructions and repeat the test.

2 Eliminating vertical blade heel
Tilt the motor counterclockwise as far as it will go in the vertical position, then lock the bevel clamp. To test for vertical heeling, position the sounding jig so that the tip of the horizontal dowel aligns with a blade tooth near the back of the table. Lower the blade and send it spinning backward so you can sample the sound as in step 1 *(right)*. Slide the yoke along the arm and repeat the process, adjusting the height if necessary; once again listen for changes in tone. If there is a discrepancy, release the yoke clamp and adjust the motor's position following the manufacturer's instructions. Retest until each test produces similar tones.

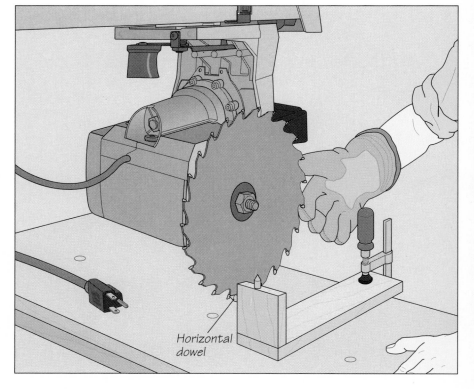

Horizontal dowel

TESTING YOUR ADJUSTMENTS

Testing the saw for square

You can check the accuracy of your adjustments to a radial arm saw much as you would for a table saw *(page 112)*. To determine whether the blade is square to the saw table, mark an X on a wide board and crosscut it at your mark. Then turn one piece over and hold the cut ends together (A in the illustration at right). Any gap between the two ends represents twice the error in the blade-to-table alignment; if necessary, repeat the adjustment shown on page 117. Now butt the two boards against the fence (B). If the two pieces do not fit together perfectly the blade is not square to the fence. Again, any gap represents twice the error; if necessary, square the blade to the fence.

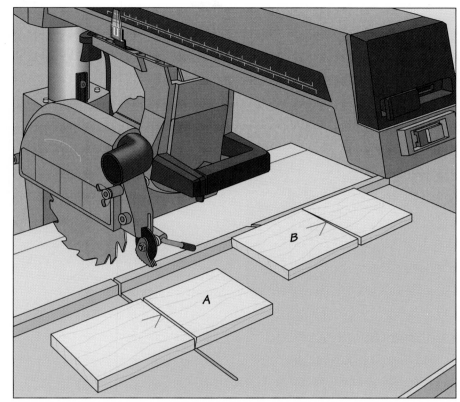

INSTALLING A FENCE AND AUXILIARY TABLE

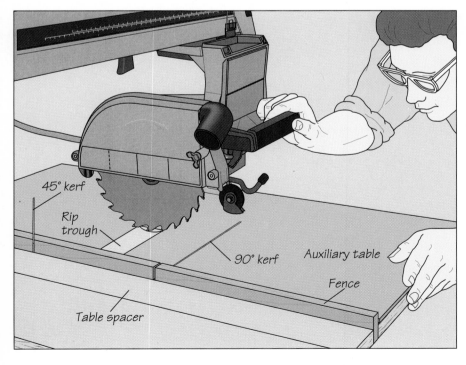

Cutting a kerf in the fence and auxiliary table

Install a fence of ¾-inch-thick, knot-free wood between the table spacer and the front table; make the fence slightly higher than the thickness of your workpiece. For an auxiliary table, cut a piece of ¼-inch hardboard or plywood the same size as the front table and use contact cement to glue it down, leaving a slight gap between it and the fence to prevent sawdust from jamming between the two. Before crosscutting or making miter cuts, slice through the fence and $\frac{1}{16}$ to ⅛ inch deep into the auxiliary table in the 90° and 45° paths of the blade. Then, raise the blade above the table and rotate the motor to the ripping position. Turn on the saw and lower it to make a $\frac{1}{16}$-inch-deep cut. Pull the yoke along the arm to furrow out a shallow rip trough in the auxiliary table.

BAND SAWS

For many woodworkers the band saw's thin, flexible blade makes it the tool of choice for cutting curves, resawing, and making fine, straight cuts. And because the blade teeth cut downward, there is no danger of kickback.

Since the band saw blade is only supported on the crown of two large

After many hours of use, the tires on band saw wheels can become worn, caked with sawdust, or stretched out of shape. If the thickness of a band saw tire is uneven around the wheel, inserting a screwdriver blade under the tire, as shown in the photo at left, and working it around the tire's circumference can restore its proper shape.

wheels, it must be properly tensioned and tracked *(page 123)* every time you change blades, otherwise you risk crooked cuts and broken blades. Setup adjustments for the machine are not time-consuming, but they are important. Particular attention should be paid to the alignment of the wheels *(page 123)*. Misaligned wheels can cause excessive blade vibration. Also periodically adjust the guide assemblies and check the table for square *(page 123)*.

If these procedures do not restore a poorly cutting saw to peak performance, the wheels or tires may be to blame. The steps shown below and on the following pages detail how to correct out-of-round and unbalanced wheels, and will make your band saw cut straighter and help its blades last longer.

CHECKING THE WHEELS

1 Checking the wheel bearings
Open one wheel cover, grasp the wheel at the sides, and rock it back and forth *(right)*. Repeat while holding the wheel at the top and bottom. If there is play in the wheel or you hear a clunking noise, remove the wheel and replace the bearing. Then repeat the test for the other wheel.

Wheel bearing

2 Testing for out-of-round wheels

Start with the upper wheel. Bracing a stick against the upper guide assembly, hold the end of the stick about $\frac{1}{16}$ inch away from the wheel's tire. Then spin the wheel by hand *(right)*. If the wheel or tire is out of round, the gap between the stick and the wheel will fluctuate; the wheel may even hit the stick. If the discrepancy exceeds $\frac{1}{32}$ inch, remedy the problem *(step 3)*. Repeat the test for the lower wheel.

Upper guide assembly

3 Fixing an out-of-round wheel

Start by determining whether the tire or the wheel itself is the problem. Try stretching the tire into shape with a screwdriver *(photo, page 120)*, then repeat the test in step 2. If the wheel is still out of round, use a sanding block to sand the tire; this may compensate for unevenness in the tire. For the lower wheel, turn on the saw and hold the sanding block against the spinning tire *(left)*. For the upper wheel, leave the saw unplugged and rotate the wheel by hand. Repeat step 2 again. If the problem persists, the wheel itself is out of round. Have it trued at a machinist's shop.

ALIGNING THE WHEELS

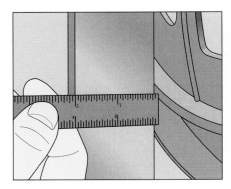

1 Checking wheel alignment
To ensure that your band saw wheels are parallel to each other and in the same vertical plane, hold a straightedge against them *(page 104)*. The straightedge should rest flush against the top and bottom of each wheel. If the wheels are out of alignment, try to bring the top wheel to a vertical position with the tilt knob. If the straightedge still will not rest flush, measure the gap between the recessed wheel and the straightedge *(above)* to determine how far you need to move the outermost wheel in *(step 2)*.

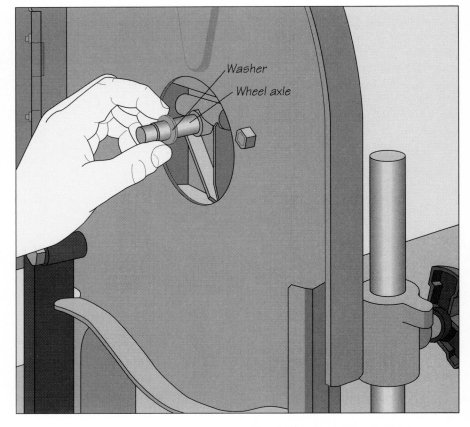

2 Shifting the outermost wheel into alignment
Remove the outermost wheel following the instructions in your owner's manual. (It is better to shift the outermost wheel in to correct the alignment rather than to move the inner wheel out; this keeps the wheels as close as possible to the saw frame.) Then shift the wheel by removing one or more of the factory-installed washers *(above)*. (If there are no washers, you can shim the recessed wheel with washers to bring the wheels into alignment.) Reinstall the wheel and tighten the axle nut. Repeat step 1.

SHOP TIP

Balancing a band saw wheel
To check the wheels of a band saw for balance, spin each one by hand. When it comes to rest, make a mark at the bottom and spin it again. If the mark comes to rest at the bottom more than two times out of three, the wheel is imbalanced. To correct the problem, drill shallow holes between the rim and spokes at the heavy point (right). Remount the wheel and perform the test again. Bore as many holes as necessary. When the wheel stops returning to the same position, it is balanced.

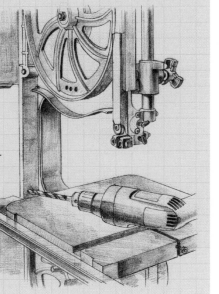

TENSIONING AND TRACKING THE BLADE

Tracking the blade

Unplug the saw and turn the tension handle at the top of the saw clockwise to raise the top wheel and increase tension on the blade. Deflect the blade from side to side to gauge the tension. Increase the tension until the blade deflects about ¼ inch to either side of the vertical. To track the blade, lower the upper guide assembly, then spin the upper wheel by hand to check whether the blade is tracking in the center of the wheel. If it is not, loosen the tilt knob lock screw. Then spin the wheel while turning the tilt knob *(right)* to angle the wheel until the blade is centered.

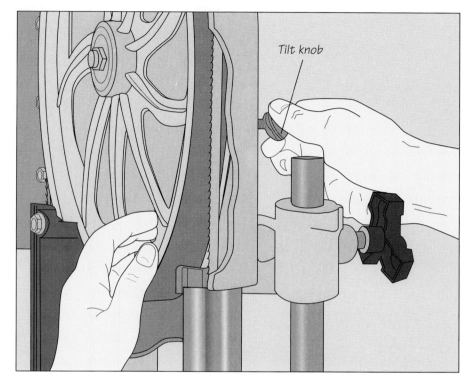

Tilt knob

ADJUSTING THE GUIDE ASSEMBLIES

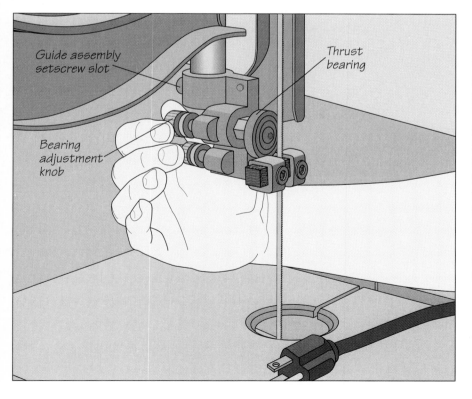

Guide assembly
setscrew slot

Thrust
bearing

Bearing
adjustment
knob

1 Setting the thrust bearings
Check by eye to see if the upper guide assembly is square to the blade. If not, loosen the guide assembly setscrew, adjust the assembly so that the bearing is square to the blade, and tighten the setscrew. Then, loosen the bearing thumbscrew and turn the adjustment knob until the thrust bearing just touches the blade. Back the bearing off slightly *(left)* and tighten the thumbscrew. The lower guide assembly thrust bearing, which is located directly beneath the table insert, is adjusted the same way. To check the setting, spin the upper wheel by hand. If the blade makes either bearing spin, back the bearing off slightly and recheck.

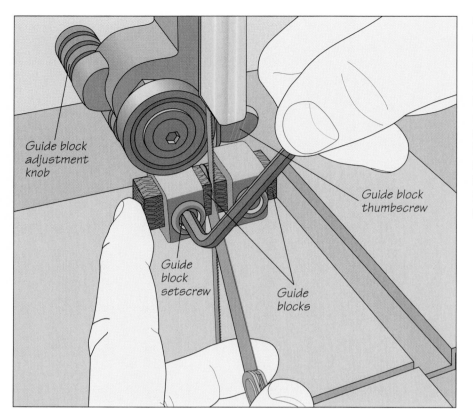

Guide block
adjustment
knob

Guide block
thumbscrew

Guide
block
setscrew

Guide
blocks

2 Setting guide blocks

To set the upper guide blocks, loosen their setscrews and pinch the blocks together using your thumb and index finger until they almost touch the blade. Alternatively, use a slip of paper or a feeler gauge *(left)* to set the space between the blocks and the blade. Tighten the setscrews. Next, loosen the thumbscrew and turn the adjustment knob until the front edges of the guide blocks are just behind the gullets. Tighten the thumbscrew. Set the lower guide blocks the same way.

SQUARING THE TABLE AND BLADE

1 Aligning the table

To ensure that the miter gauge slot is properly aligned on both sides of the table slot, set the miter gauge in its slot and slide the gauge back and forth across the table. The gauge should slide freely with only moderate pressure. If the gauge binds, use locking pliers to remove the alignment pin. Then, insert the pin into its hole and use a ball-peen hammer to tap it deeper *(right)* until the miter gauge slides freely.

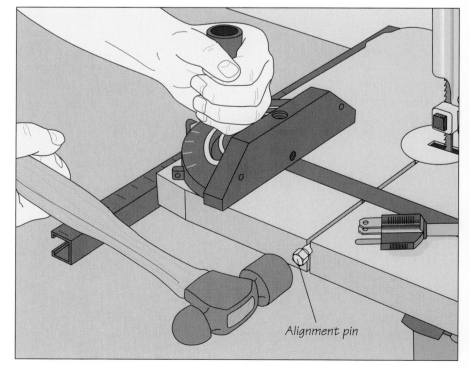

Alignment pin

2 Checking the table angle

With the table in the horizontal position, remove the table insert, then butt a combination square against the side of the saw blade as shown. The square should fit flush against the table and blade *(right)*. If there is a gap between the two, loosen the two table lock knobs underneath the table and make sure the table is seated properly on the table stop. Tighten the lock knobs. If the gap remains, adjust the table stop *(step 3)*.

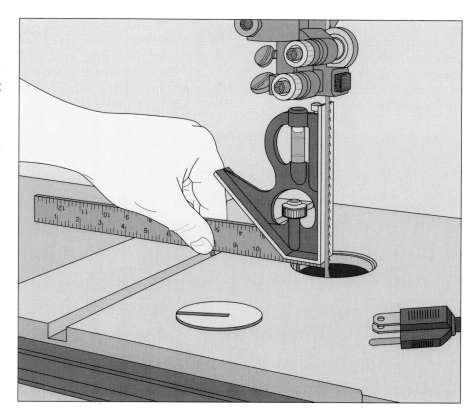

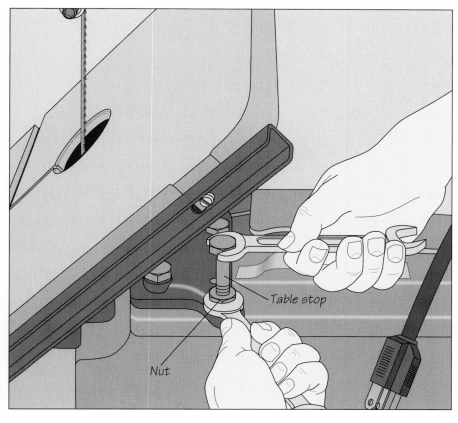

3 Aligning the table stop

Tilt the table out of the way, then use two wrenches as shown to adjust the table stop. Use the lower wrench to hold the lock nut stationary and the upper wrench to turn the table stop *(left)*. Turn the stop clockwise to lower it and counterclockwise to raise it. Recheck the table angle.

JOINTERS AND PLANERS

The team of jointer and thickness planer are responsible for squaring the edges and faces of a workpiece. The success of any woodworking project rests on these first crucial steps, so it is essential that both machines are set up properly. Even the most accurate table saw will only compound errors made at the jointing and planing stage.

Accurate jointing depends on precise alignment of the two tables and the fence. Begin by ensuring that the outfeed table is at the same height as the cutting edges of the knives at their highest point, also known as Top Dead Center or TDC (below). Then check that the tables are perfectly square to the fence and aligned with each other (page 127).

Because it has more moving parts, the thickness planer requires a little more attention. Most importantly, always check to see that the feed rollers are properly adjusted (page 129) and that the planer's bed is parallel to the cutterhead along its length (page 130).

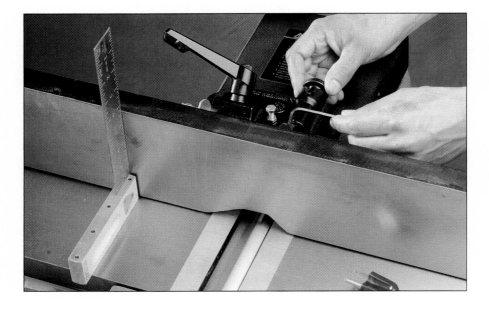

Most jointers have 90° positive stops that can be fine-tuned if the fence cannot be accurately squared to the table through normal adjustment. For the model shown (left), *the 90° positive stop is a spring-loaded plunger that sits in an index collar. To fine-tune the fence position, the index collar is adjusted by means of a setscrew.*

SETTING OUTFEED TABLE HEIGHT

1 Checking table height
With the jointer unplugged, use a small wooden wedge to rotate the cutterhead until the edge of one knife is at its highest point. Then hold a straight hardwood board on the outfeed table so that it extends over the cutterhead without contacting the infeed table *(right)*. The knife should just brush against the board. Perform the test along the length of the knife, moving the board from the fence to the rabbeting ledge. Repeat the test for the other knives. If a knife fails the test, adjust its height *(page 84)*. If none of the knives is level with the board, raise or lower the outfeed table by loosening the table lock and moving the outfeed table adjustment handle.

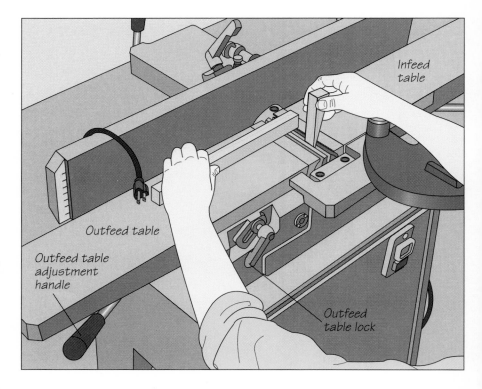

Infeed table

Outfeed table

Outfeed table adjustment handle

Outfeed table lock

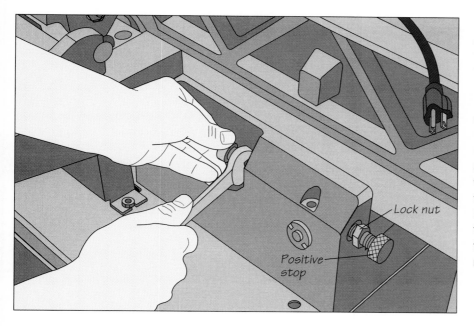

2 Adjusting the positive stop

If the outfeed table is still not level with the knives, adjust the jointer's positive stops, which prevent the table from moving out of alignment while in use. For the model shown, first tighten the outfeed table lock and loosen the two lock nuts on the other side of the tool. Back off the two positive stops and then adjust the height of the outfeed table with the adjustment handle *(step 1)* until the table is level with the knives at their highest point of rotation. Tighten the table lock. Tighten the positive stops as far as they will go, then tighten the lock nuts *(left)*.

ALIGNING THE TABLES AND FENCE

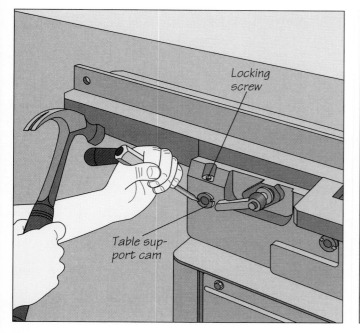

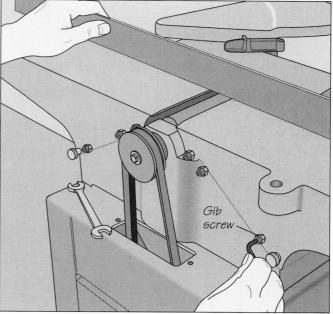

1 Aligning the tables

Remove the jointer's fence, then raise the infeed table to the same height as the outfeed table. Use a straightedge to confirm that the two tables are absolutely level. If the alignment is not perfect, adjust the horizontal position of the tables. The model shown features eccentric table supports that can be adjusted by first loosening a locking screw and then tapping an adjustment cam with a hammer and screwdriver *(above, left)*.

When the tables are perfectly level, tighten the locking screws. If you have a jointer with gib screws, adjust one or more of the gib screws at the back of the tool until the straightedge rests flush on both tables *(above, right)*; remove the pulley cover, if necessary, to access the screws. If you moved the outfeed table during this process, recheck its height *(page 126)*.

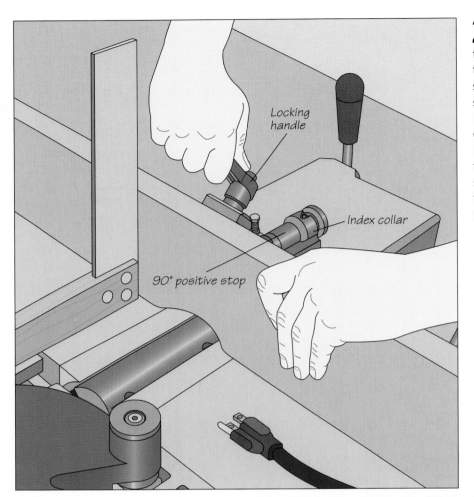

2 Squaring the fence with the tables
With the fence set in its vertical position, hold a try square on the outfeed table near the cutterhead and butt the square's blade against the fence. The square should fit flush against the fence. If there is any gap between the two, slacken the locking handle, tilt the fence until it is flush with the square, and retighten the handle *(left)*. The 90° positive stop should be engaged in the index collar. If the fence is still out-of-square, adjust the positive stop *(page 126)*.

One of the most common jointing and planing defects is snipe, or a concave cut at the trailing end of a workpiece. On a planer, snipe occurs when there is too much play between the table and the feed rollers, and can be corrected by proper feed roller adjustment (page 129). On a jointer (right), snipe occurs when the outfeed table is set lower than the knives at their highest point of rotation, and can be corrected by aligning the outfeed table (page 126).

PLANERS

Cleaning planer rollers

Planer feed rollers can get dirty quickly when planing pitch-filled softwoods such as pine. Periodically use mineral spirits or a solution of ammonia and water with a brass-bristled brush to clean metal feed rollers of pitch and resin. Clean rubber feed rollers with a sharp cabinet scraper *(right)*.

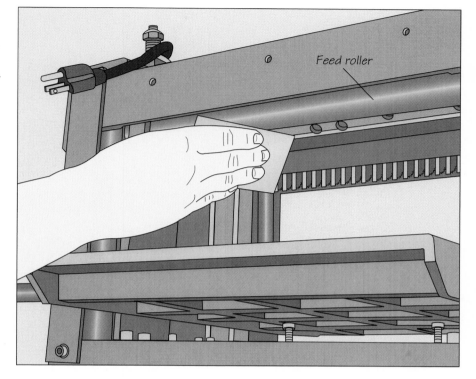

Feed roller

Adjustment nut

Adjusting feed rollers

Sometimes it is necessary to increase pressure on a planer's feed rollers, as when planing narrow stock or when stock slips as it is fed into the machine. In either case, the infeed roller should firmly grip the board. (Some planers feature a serrated metal infeed roller; in this case the pressure should be enough to move the board but not so much that the rollers leave a serrated pattern in the board after it is planed.) On most planers, the feed rollers are adjusted by turning spring-loaded screws on top of the machine. For the model shown, remove the plastic caps and adjust the hex nuts with an open-end wrench *(left)*. Make sure after adjusting the feed rollers that the table is parallel to the rollers *(page 130)*. If the rollers do not carry the wood smoothly through the planer after adjustments, clean the rollers or wax the table.

Checking the table for level
To check if your planer's table is level and parallel to the cutterhead, run two jointed strips of wood of the same thickness through opposite sides of the machine *(left)*, then compare the resulting thicknesses. If there is a measurable difference, adjust the table according to the manufacturer's instructions. If your model of planer has no such adjustment, reset the knives in the cutterhead so that they are slightly lower at the lower end of the table to compensate for the error.

Lubricating the height adjustment
To ensure smooth operation, periodically clean the planer's height adjustment mechanism, first using a clean, dry cloth to remove sawdust and grease. Then lubricate the threads with a Teflon™-based lubricant or automotive bearing grease; oil should be avoided as it may stain the wood.

DRILL PRESSES

Drill presses have a reputation as workhorse machines that rarely—if ever—require maintenance. And yet they can slip out of alignment just as easily as any other stationary power tool.

Most drill press problems are found in the chuck and table. A table that is not square to the spindle is the most common problem, and is easily remedied. Runout, or wobble, is a more serious problem, and can be traced to the spindle or chuck. If the problem lies with the spindle, it can often be fixed simply by striking the spindle with a hammer until it is true; if the chuck is at fault, it must be removed and replaced.

Do not neglect the drill press' belts and pulleys in your maintenance. Check the belts for wear, and always keep them tensioned properly. Periodically check the bearings in the pulleys, and replace them if they become worn.

The speed of many drill presses is changed by a system of belts and pulleys housed in the top of the tool. To keep the belts at the proper degree of tension, these drill presses feature a lever that loosens the belts for changing and tightens them to set the correct tension (right). A belt should flex about 1 inch out of line.

SQUARING THE TABLE

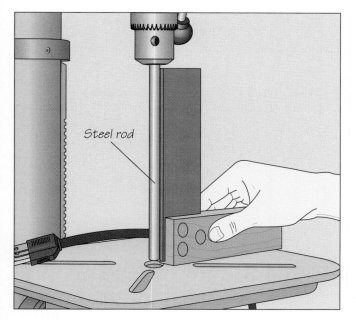

1 Aligning the table
Install an 8-inch-long steel rod in the drill press chuck as you would a drill bit, then raise the table until it almost touches the rod. Butt a try square against the rod as shown; the blade should rest flush against it *(above)*. If there is a gap, adjust the table following the manufacturer's instructions. For the model shown, remove the alignment pin under the table, loosen the table locking bolt, and swivel the table until the rod is flush with the square. Tighten the locking bolt.

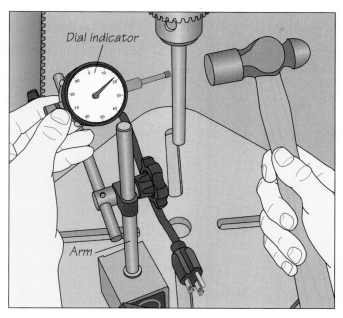

2 Correcting chuck runout
Use a dial indicator to see if there is any runout, or wobble, in the chuck *(page 105)*. If there is, rap the rod with a ball-peen hammer *(above)* and then measure for runout again; 0.005 inch is considered the maximum acceptable amount. Pull the arm of the dial indicator out of the way each time you tap the rod.

REPLACING THE CHUCK

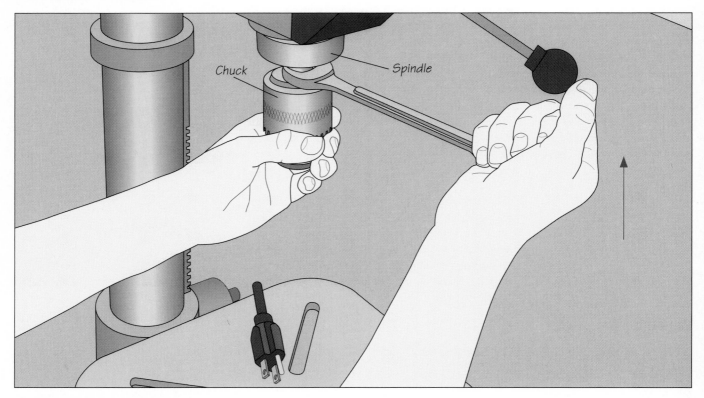

Chuck   Spindle

Removing and remounting a chuck

Chucks are commonly attached to the quill of a drill press with a tapered spindle. (Older models often have chucks that are simply screwed in place.) To remove a faulty chuck that features a tapered spindle, first lower the quill and lock it in place. Fit an open-end wrench around the spindle on top of the chuck and give the wrench a sharp upward blow *(above)*. The chuck should slide out. If not, rotate the spindle and try again. To remount the chuck, press-fit it into the spindle by hand. Then, with the chuck's jaws fully retracted, give the chuck a sharp blow with a wooden mallet.

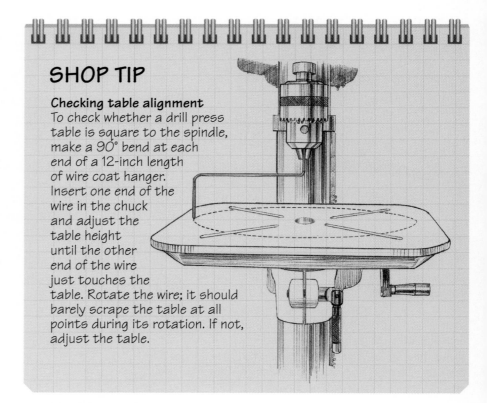

SHOP TIP

Checking table alignment
To check whether a drill press table is square to the spindle, make a 90° bend at each end of a 12-inch length of wire coat hanger. Insert one end of the wire in the chuck and adjust the table height until the other end of the wire just touches the table. Rotate the wire; it should barely scrape the table at all points during its rotation. If not, adjust the table.

LATHES AND SHAPERS

The drive centers of a lathe should be kept as sharp as your turning tools. If the spurs or point of a drive center are dull or chipped, they will not grip the workpiece properly. Drive centers are sharpened on a bench grinder or with a file (right). A 35° bevel on the underside of each spur works best.

LATHES

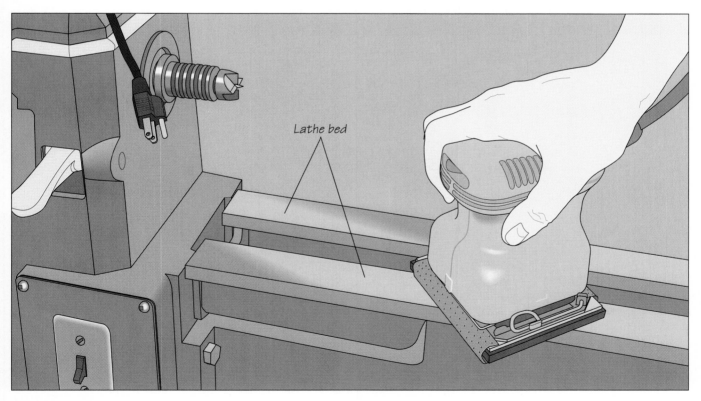

Lathe bed

Sanding the lathe bed

If your shop is in a humid climate, the bed of your lathe may develop a thin layer of rust which can prevent the tailstock and tool rest from sliding smoothly. To keep the lathe bed clean, remove any rust as soon as it appears by sanding the bed with fine sandpaper *(above)*, 200-grit or finer, then apply a paste wax.

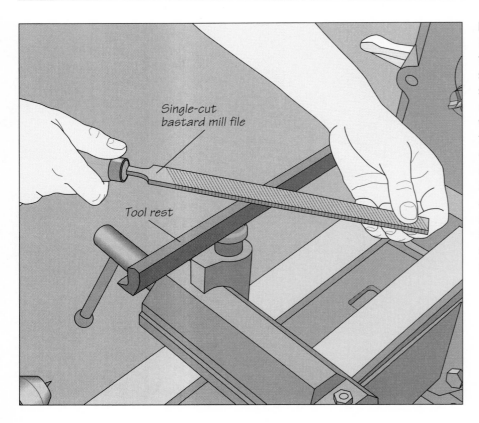

Draw-filing the tool rest
Because it is made of softer steel than the turning tools used against it, the bearing surface of the tool rest will develop low spots, marks, and nicks with constant use. If not remedied, these imperfections will be transferred to the workpieces you turn, or cause the tool to skip. You can re-dress a tool rest easily with a single-cut bastard mill file. Draw-file the rest by hold-ing the file at an angle and pushing it across the work from right to left in over-lapping strokes *(left)*. Continue until you have removed the nicks and hollows, then smooth the surface with 200-grit sandpa-per or emery cloth.

Checking for center alignment
Turning between centers requires precise alignment of drive centers between head-stock and tailstock, otherwise you will produce off-center turnings. To see if the drive centers line up, insert a four-spur drive center in the headstock and a live center in the tailstock. Slide the tailstock along the bed up to the headstock *(right)*. The points of the drive centers should meet exactly. If they do not, you may have to shim the tailstock or file down its base.

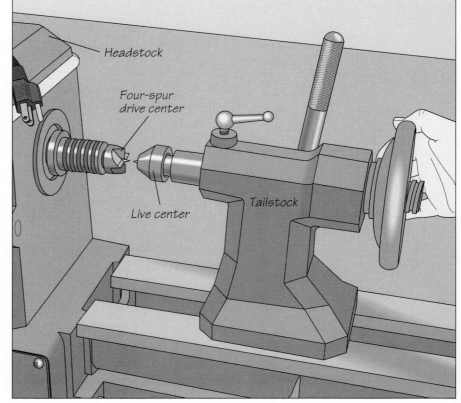

SHAPERS

Checking for spindle runout

Set a magnetic-base dial indicator face up on the shaper table so the plunger of the device contacts the spindle. Calibrate the gauge to zero following the manufacturer's instructions. Then turn the spindle slowly by hand *(right)*. The dial indicator will register spindle runout—the amount of wobble that the spindle will transfer to the cutter. Perform the test at intervals along the length of the spindle, adjusting its height ½ inch at a time. If the runout exceeds 0.005 inch for any of the tests, replace the spindle.

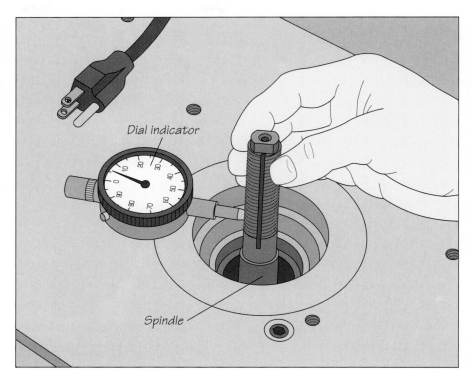

Dial indicator

Spindle

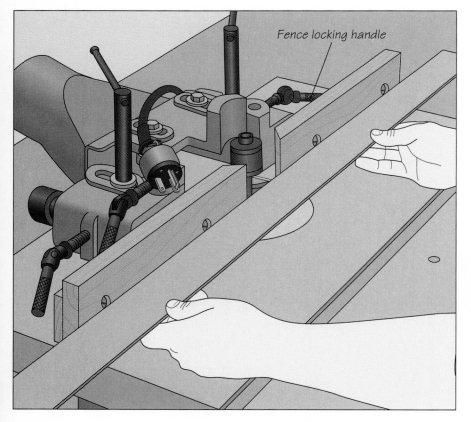

Fence locking handle

Squaring the fences

The two halves of a shaper fence—or a router table fence—must be perfectly parallel, otherwise your cuts will be uneven. To square the fences on a shaper, first loosen the fence locking handles. Hold a straightedge against the fences. The two halves should butt against the straightedge *(left)*. If not, add wood shims behind the fences until they are parallel.

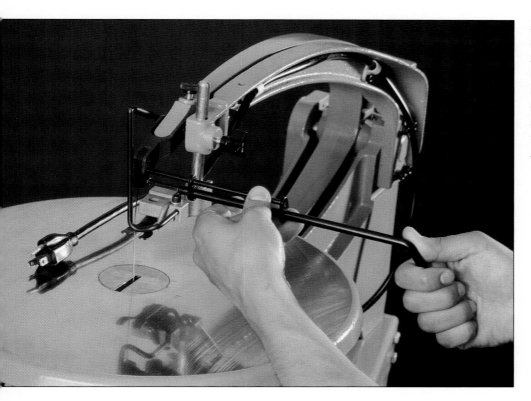

Because a scroll saw blade is held in clamps that pivot on the end of the saw's arms during a cut, replacing a blade is a tricky task that risks stretching and snapping the delicate cutting edge. The model of scroll saw shown at left features a unique blade-changing wrench that holds the blade clamps steady as the blade is tightened.

SCROLL SAWS

Checking blade tension

The blades of a scroll saw—like those of a band saw—require proper tension to cut effectively. Too little tension will cause excessive vibration and allow the blade to wander during the cut. Too much tension can lead to blade breakage. To adjust blade tension on the model shown, first tilt the blade tension lever forward. Then adjust the blade tension knob *(right)* to increase or decrease blade tension. Tilt the blade tension lever back and test the blade. It should deflect about ⅛ inch when pushed from side to side. Pluck the blade and remember the sound. It will allow you to tension the blade quickly in future. Always adjust the tension when you change blades.

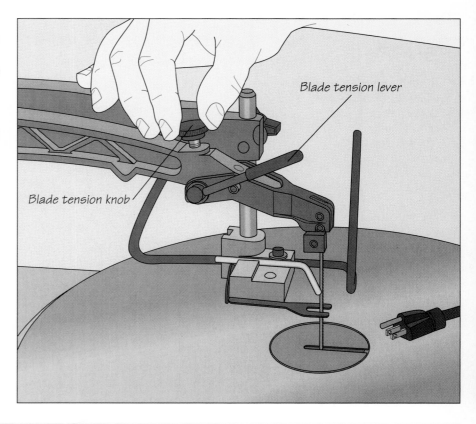

Blade tension lever

Blade tension knob

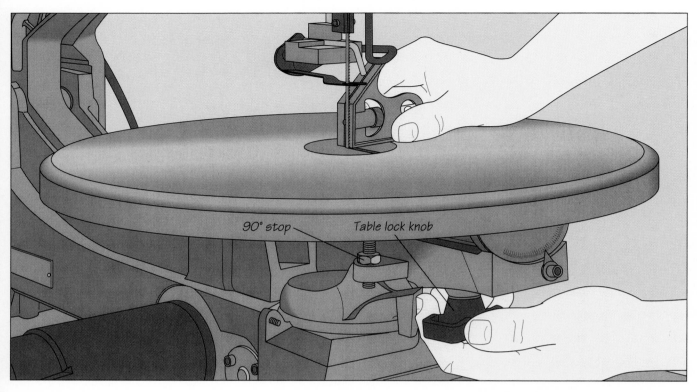

90° stop   Table lock knob

Squaring the blade

To square the scroll saw's blade to the table, butt a combination square against the blade as shown. The square should fit flush against the blade. If there is a gap, loosen the table lock knob and adjust the nut on the 90° stop until the table is level and there is no gap between the square and the blade. Tighten the lock knob *(above)*.

SHOP TIP

Installing an air pump

Older scroll saws and some foreign models often come without a sawdust blower, a device that keeps the cutting line clear while the saw is in use. A simple electric aquarium pump and some copper tubing *(right)* can do the trick at a fraction of the cost

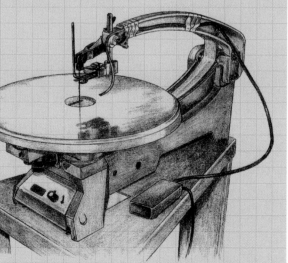

of a sawdust blowing attachment. Simply insert a 10- to 12-inch length of copper tubing into the pump's plastic air hose, making an airtight seal. Tape the hose to the saw's upper arm, and bend the copper end to point at the blade. Pinch the end of the tube slightly to direct the air and increase its pressure.

BELT-AND-DISC SANDERS

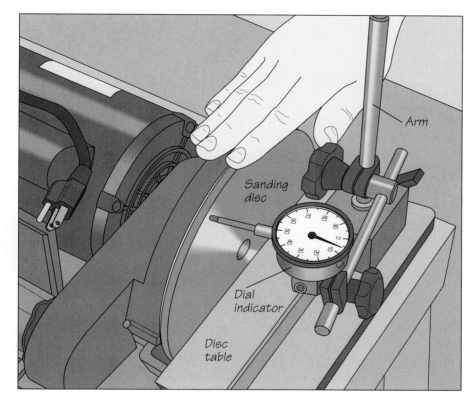

Sanding disc

Arm

Dial indicator

Disc table

Testing for trueness

To measure whether the wheel is true, first remove any abrasive discs. Connect a dial indicator to a magnetic base and set the base on the tool's disc table. Place the device so that its arm contacts the disc and turn on the magnet. Calibrate the dial indicator to zero following the manufacturer's instructions. Turn the sanding disc by hand, and read the result *(left)*. The dial indicator will register the trueness of the wheel. Perform the test at various points around the disc. If the amount of wobble exceeds 0.005 inch for any of the tests, adjust the motor position or have the bearings replaced.

Tracking the sanding belt

To straighten a sanding belt that is not tracking true, turn the belt-and-disc sander's tracking knob clockwise or counterclockwise while the tool is running *(right)*. To correct severe tracking problems, unplug the tool and release tension on the sanding belt by pushing down on the tracking knob. Center the belt on the pulleys and release the knob. Then turn on the tool and adjust the tracking knob as required. Always track the belt when changing belts or installing a new one.

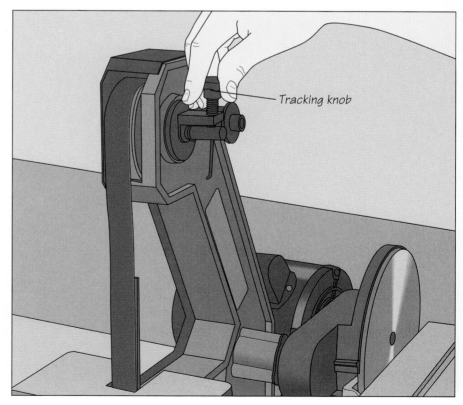

Tracking knob

AIR COMPRESSORS

Draining the compressor

When an air compressor has been used for an extended period of time or in exceedingly humid conditions, moisture will collect in the tank. This moisture may cause rust; it can also be sprayed out with the air, which can ruin a spray lacquer finish. To drain the moisture, shut off the motor, relieve all pressure from the tank, and open the drainage valve at the bottom *(right)*. Drain the tank periodically, depending on how often you use the compressor.

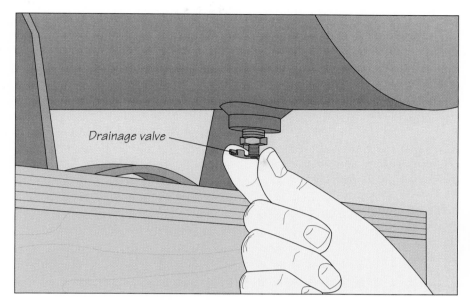

Drainage valve

Changing the oil and air filters

After every 100 hours of operation, change an air compressor's oil. To drain the oil, shut off the motor, relieve all pressure from the tank, and loosen the drain plug with a wrench. Collect the old oil in a container and dispose of it safely. Close the drain plug and fill the pump with the oil recommended by the manufacturer *(left)*. Do not overfill the pump. Also check the air filter weekly. To clean the air filter, remove the housing and lift off the filter *(inset)*. Clean the filter in a solution of detergent and water; replace it if it cannot be cleaned.

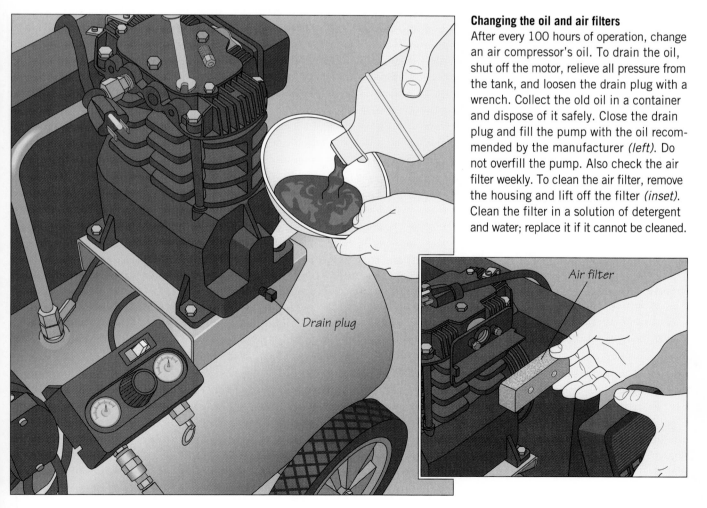

Drain plug

Air filter

GLOSSARY

Abrasive: A coarse powder or a piece of paper or fabric coated with grit particles used to smooth wood.

Arbor: A shaft driven by a stationary power tool motor to turn a revolving blade or other cutting implement.

Bearing: A machined part located on a motor shaft, permitting the shaft to turn without friction.

Belt tension: The measure of how tight a stationary power tool drive belt or abrasive belt is stretched across its pulleys.

Benchstone: Any natural or synthetic sharpening stone used at the bench.

Bevel cut: Sawing at an angle from face to face through a workpiece.

Blade heel: Blade rotation that is not perfectly parallel to the fence of a table saw, or the arm of a radial arm saw.

Blade set: The amount that saw teeth are alternately offset to left and right, allowing a blade to cut a kerf slightly wider than its own thickness to help prevent binding.

Blade tension: The measure of how tight a band saw blade is stretched across its wheels.

Brushes: A carbon or copper conductor that delivers current from the stationary element of an electric motor to the rotating coil.

Buffing: Polishing a sharpened edge to a mirror-like finish using a cloth or rubber wheel impregnated with fine abrasive compounds.

Burnisher: A rod-like steel tool used to turn a lip on a tool edge, especially scraper edges.

Burr: A small ridge formed on the flat face of a tool blade as a result of the honing process.

Cap iron: A metal plate screwed to a plane blade, preventing chatter and the buildup of wood chips.

Carbide-tipped blade: A saw blade on which the teeth are made of a compound of carbon and steel; such blade edges are stronger and stay sharper longer than conventional high-speed steel blades.

Chip lifter: The machined surfaces on a Fortsner or multi-spur bit directly behind the cutters.

Chuck: Adjustable jaws on a drill or drill press for holding bits or other accessories.

Collet: The sleeve that grips the shank of a router bit.

Combination blade: A circular saw blade designed for making both crosscuts and rip cuts.

Crosscut: A cut made across the grain of a workpiece.

D-E-F-G-H-I

Dado head: A blade, or combination of blades and chippers, used to cut dadoes in wood.

Dado: A rectangular channel cut into a workpiece.

Dial indicator: A measuring device with a magnetic base used to determine runout on stationary and portable power tools, typically calibrated in thousandths of an inch.

Drill point angle: The angle to which a drill bit must be ground and sharpened for efficient cutting.

Drive belt: Any rubber belt that connects a stationary power tool motor with its arbor or spindle, sometimes through a system of pulleys.

Drive center: A lathe accessory mounted in either the tailstock or headstock to support turning work; can either be fixed or turn with the work by means of ball-bearings.

Feeler gauge: A precisely ground metal blade, furnished in sets, used to accurately measure the gap between tool parts.

Fence: An adjustable guide designed to keep the edge or face of a workpiece a set distance from the cutting edge of a tool.

Ferrule: A metal ring that tightens around the end of a handle to prevent splitting.

Frog: The part of a hand plane that supports the blade; usually the frog can be moved back and forth to adjust the mouth opening of the plane.

Grinding: The initial step in sharpening where nicks are removed, the cutting edge is squared, and the bevel is established; typically done on a bench grinder.

Gullet: The gap between teeth on a saw blade.

Honing: The process of converting a rough-ground edge to a smooth, uniform cutting edge.

Hook: A uniform burr turned on the cutting edges of a scraper.

Infeed: The part of a machine's table that is in front of the blade during a cutting operation.

J-K-L-M-N-O-P-Q

Jointing: Cutting thin shavings from the edge and face of a workpiece until they are flat and square.

Kerf: The space left when wood is removed by the saw blade.

Kickback: The tendency of a workpiece to be thrown back in the direction of the operator of a tool.

Lapping: Rubbing the face of a plane or chisel blade across a sharpening stone to remove the burr that results from honing the blade.

Microbevel: A secondary bevel honed on the cutting edge of a blade.

Miter cut: A cut that angles across the face of a workpiece.

Oilstone: Any natural or synthetic sharpening stone that uses oil as a lubricant.

Orbital action: The up-and-forward movement of some saber saw blades on their upstroke; replaces the traditional straight up-and-down action of a reciprocating-type saber saw. Also, the eccentric motion of the abrasive disc on an orbital or random-orbit sander.

Out-of-round wheel: A band saw wheel that is not perfectly round.

Outfeed: The part of a machine's table that is behind the blade during a cutting operation.

Platen: A support plate for sandpaper belts on sanders.

Positive stop: An adjustable screw on a stationary power tool used to keep the tool's table at a set angle, typically 90° and 45°.

Quill: A sleeve surrounding the spindle of a drill press; the amount that the quill can be raised and lowered determines the depth of hole a drill press can bore.

R-S

Raker: A tooth in a saw blade that clears sawdust and wood chips out of the kerf.

Reverse thread: A machined thread that tightens and loosens in the opposite direction to the rotation of the tool bit so that the cutter remains tight during operation.

Rip cut: A cut that follows the grain of a workpiece—usually made along its length.

Runout: The amount of wobble in tool's arbor or spindle.

Sharp: A cutting edge is said to be sharp where two flat, polished surfaces meet at an angle.

Slipstone: A sharpening stone with curved edges used to sharpen gouges and other similarly shaped tools.

Snipe: A concave cut created by a jointer or planer at the end of a workpiece, the result of improper pressure on the workpiece or inaccurately set table height.

Spindle: The threaded arbor on a power tool that turns cutters and accessories.

Square: Two surfaces of a workpiece that are at 90° to each other.

Stropping: Polishing a sharpened edge to a mirror-like finish using strips of leather impregnated with fine abrasive compounds.

T-U-V-W-X-Y-Z

Tearout: The tendency of a blade or cutter to tear the fibers of wood, leaving ragged edges on the surface of the workpiece.

Teeth per inch (TPI): A unit of measurement used to identify types and uses of saw blades by the number of teeth per inch of blade length.

Temper: The degree of hardness in tool steel; also, the color of steel after the tempering process.

Tracking: Adjusting a band saw blade or abrasive belt so that it is centered on the tool's wheels.

Waterstone: Any natural or synthetic sharpening stone that uses water as a lubricant.

Wheel dresser: A device used to true the working surface of a grinding wheel and expose fresh abrasive.

INDEX

Page references in *italics* indicate an illustration of subject matter. Page references in **bold** indicate a Build It Yourself project.

A-B-C-D

Abrasives, *back endpaper*
Adzes, *51, 53, 54*
Air compressors, *139*
Air pumps:
  Scroll saws, *137*
Axes, *51, 54*
  Choosing a durable ax handle (Shop Tip), *54*
Band saws:
  Blades, *123*
    repairing broken blades, *76-77*
    rounding a band saw blade (Shop Tip), *75*
    sharpening, *73-74*
    storage, *78*
  Guide assemblies, *123-124*
  Heat-resistant guide blocks, *59, 75*
  Table alignment, *124-125*
  Wheels, *120-121*
    alignment, *104, 122*
    balancing a band saw wheel (Shop Tip), *122*
Belt sanders, *88*
Bench grinders, *16, 20, 21*
  Grinding jigs, *13*
  Multi-tool jigs, *16*
  Reversing wheel guards for buffing (Shop Tip), *22*
  Wheels
    dressing, *22*
    identification, 20
Bench planes, *39*
  Assembly and adjustment, *39, 45*
  Blades
    grinding with a sander (Shop Tip), *42*
    honing guide and angle jigs, *17*
    sharpening, *41-44*
    squaring, *13*
  Refurbishing, *40-41*
Benchstones, 13
  Oilstones, *18*
  Truing, *19*
  Waterstones, *12, 17, 18, 19*
Bevels, *back endpaper*
  Microbevels, *15*
Bits, *60*
  Drills
    auger bits, *55-57*
    brad-point bits, *68-69*
    drill bit grinding attachments, *58, 61*
    drill bit sharpening jigs, *61, 66*
    Forstner bits, *67*

  multi-spur bits, *68*
  spade bits, *69*
  spoon bits, *55, 57*
  storage, *89*
  twist bits, *58, 65-66*
  Routers
    non-piloted bits, *62*
    piloted bits, *63*
    router bit sharpeners, *61*
    storage, *89*
  Storing bits (Shop Tip), *89*
Blades, *60*
  Band saws, *123*
  Bench planes, *13, 17, 41-44*
  Circular saws, *61 72, 86*
  Radial arm saws, *64, 113, 117, 118, 119*
  Saber saws, *93*
  Scroll saws, *136-137*
  Shapers, *62, 63*
  Table saws, *64, 70, 109*
  See also Knives
Braces, *55-57*
Brush assemblies, *98*
Build It Yourself:
  Hand tools
    bench vise saw holders, **28**
    gouge-sharpening jigs, **33**
  Mobile sharpening dollies, **23**
Chisels:
  Handles, *31*
  Sharpening, *32*
Circular saws, *88, 97*
  Blades
    alignment, *86*
    blade-setting jigs, *61, 72*
    blade-sharpening jigs, *61, 72*
    changing, *71*
    cleaning, *71*
    sharpening, *72*
Compressors, *139*
Disc-and-belt sanders, *138-139*
Drawknives, *24, 51, 53, 54*
Dressers, *16, 22*
Drill presses, *131*
  Chucks, *131-132*
  Runout, *105*
  Table alignment, *131*
    checking table alignment (Shop Tip), *132*
Drills, *88, 95*
  Bits
    auger bits, *55-57*
    bit grinding attachments, *58, 61*
    brad-point bits, *68-69*
    Forstner bits, *67*
    multi-spur bits, *68*
    sharpening jigs, *61, 66*

  spade bits, *69*
  spoon bits, *55, 57*
  storage, *89*
  twist bits, *58, 65-66*
  See also Drill presses

E-F-G-H

Electrical outlets, *front endpaper*
Electric drills. *See* Drills
Extension cords, 89
Files, *17*
Gouges, *25, 30*
  Handles, *31*
  Sharpening
    carving gouges, *36-37*
    gouge-sharpening jigs, **33**
    roughing-out gouges, *33-34*
    spindle gouges, *35*
    v-tools, *38*
  Shop-made honing guides and rust removers (Shop Tip), *34*
Grinders. *See* Bench grinders
Grinding, 15
Handsaws:
  Bench vise saw holders, **28**
  Filing, *26-27, 29*
  Jointing, *29*
  Setting, *26, 29*
  Storage
    saw holders (Shop Tip), *27*
Hand tools, *25*
  Drills, *55-57*
  Roughing and shaping tools, *51-54*
  See also Bench planes; Chisels; Gouges; Handsaws; Scrapers
Hatchets. *See* Axes
Honing, 15

I-J-K-L

Inshaves, *51, 53, 54*
Jigs:
  Grinders
    grinding jigs, *13*
    multi-tool jigs, *16*
  Hand tools
    gouge-sharpening jigs, **28**
    handsaws, **28**
  Plane honing guide and angle jigs, *17*
  Routers
    plywood truing jigs, *87*
  Sharpening power tools
    circular saw blade-setting jigs, *61, 72*
    circular saw blade-sharpening jigs, *61, 72*
    drill bit grinding attachments, *58, 61*
    drill bit sharpening jigs, *61, 66*
    jointer/planer knife-setting jigs, *61, 79*

Jointer/planer knife-sharpening jigs, *61, 82-83*
  planer/jointer magnetic knife-setting jigs, *79, 85*
  twist bit sharpening jigs, *66*
Jointers, *126*
  Knife-setting jigs, *61, 79*
  Knife-sharpening jigs, *61, 82-83*
  Knives
    bevels, *back endpaper*
    installation, *85*
    sharpening, *79-84*
    shifting knives for longer life (Shop Tip), *81*
  Positive stops, *126, 127*
  Snipe, *128*
  Table alignment, *127-128*
  Table height, *126*
Knives:
  Jointers
    bevels, *back endpaper*
    installation, *85*
    knife-setting jigs, *61, 79*
    knife-sharpening jigs, *61, 82-83*
    sharpening, *79-84*
    shifting knives for longer life (Shop Tip), *81*
  Molding knives, *64*
  Planers
    bevels, *back endpaper*
    knife-setting jigs, *61, 79*
    knife-sharpening jigs, *61, 82-83*
Lapping, *15*
Lathes, *133-134*
Lowe, Philip, *8-9*

M-N-O-P-Q
Microbevels, *15*
Oilstones, *18*
Orbital sanders, *88*
Planers, *126*
  Cleaning, *129, 130*
  Knives
    bevels, *back endpaper*
    knife-setting jigs, *61, 79*
    knife-sharpening jigs, *61, 82-83*
    sharpening, *79, 85*
  Rollers, *129*
  Table alignment, *130*
Planes. *See* Bench planes
Plate joiners, *88, 94*
Plugs, *102-103*
Polishing, *15*
Power tools:
  Brush assemblies, *98*
  Drive belts, *106*

Electrical supply, *front endpaper*, 89
  cords, *100-101*
  plugs, *102-103*
  switches, *99, 107*
  wattage ratings, *front endpaper*
Lathes, *133-134*
Maintenance, 8, *87-89*, 105
Plate joiners, 88
Safety precautions, *front endpaper*, 98
  disabling a power tool (Shop Tip), *103*
Scroll saws, *136-137*
  installing an air pump (Shop Tip), *137*
Shapers, 62, *135*
  storage racks for shaper cutters (Shop Tip), *63*
Tables, *107*
See also Band saws; Bench grinders; Circular saws; Drill presses; Drills; Jointers; Planers; Radial arm saws; Routers; Saber saws; Sanders; Table saws

R-S-T-U-V
Radial arm saws, 113
  Auxiliary tables, *119*
  Blades
    blade heel, *113, 118*
    squaring, *117, 119*
  Clamps, *114-115*
  Cleaning, *113*
  Fences, *119*
  Molding knives, *64*
  Sliding mechanisms, *113, 116*
  Table adjustment, *114*
Routers, 88, *90, 98*
  Bits, *62-63*
    router bit sharpeners, *61*
    storage, *89*
  Collet runout, *91*
  Sub-bases
    truing, *87*
Saber saws, 88, *92*
  Blades
    extending blade life (Shop Tip), *93*
    squaring, *93*
Safety precautions:
  Power tools, *front endpaper, 98*
    disabling a power tool (Shop Tip), *103*
Sanders, 88, *96*
  Disc-and-belt sanders, *138-139*
Scrapers, *46*
  Bevels, *back endpaper*
  Sharpening
    cabinet scrapers, *46, 48-50*
    handscrapers, *46, 47-48*
    maintaining the correct burnishing angle (Shop Tip), *50*

Scroll saws:
  Blades, *136-137*
  Installing an air pump (Shop Tip), *137*
Shapers, 62, *135*
  Storage racks for shaper cutters (Shop Tip), *63*
Sharpening stones. *see* Benchstones
Sharpening techniques, 6, 11, *13-15*
Sharpening tools, *16-17*
  Belt sanders
    grinding with a sander (Shop Tip), *42*
  Burnishers, *46*
    maintaining the correct burnishing angle (Shop Tip), *50*
    variable burnishers, *46*
  Dressers, 16, *22*
  Mobile sharpening dollies, **23**
  For power tools, *61*
  See also Bench grinders; Benchstones
Shop Tips:
  Hand tools, *27, 34, 42, 50, 54*
  Portable power tools, *22, 89, 93, 103*
  Stationary power tools, *63, 75, 81, 110, 122, 132, 137*
Spokeshaves, *51, 52, 54*
Starr, Richard, *6-7*
Stones. *see* Benchstones
Strops, *back endpaper*, 17
Switches, *99, 107*
Table saws:
  Blades
    angle adjustment, *109*
    changing, *70*
    storage, *70*
  Cleaning, *108, 112*
  Height and tilt mechanisms, *112*
  Miter gauges
    fixing a loose miter gauge (Shop Tip), *110*
    squaring, *110*
  Molding knives, *64*
  Rip fences, *111*
  Table alignment, *108-109, 111*
  Table inserts, *112*
Tip burning, 11
Tools. *See* Hand tools; Power tools; Sharpening tools
Twist bits:
  Bevels, *back endpaper*

W-X-Y-Z
Waterstones, 18, *19*
  Japanese finish stones, *12*, 18, *19*
  Storage units, *17*
Waymark, Ian, *10-11*
Wet/dry grinders, 16, *20, 21*

ACKNOWLEDGMENTS

The editors wish to thank the following:

SHARPENING BASICS
Cooper Tools, Apex, NC; Delta International Machinery/Porter Cable, Guelph, Ont.; Diamond Machinery Technology Inc., Marlborough, MA; Garrett Wade Company, New York, NY; Lee Valley Tools Ltd., Ottawa, Ont; Record Tools Inc., Pickering, Ont.; The Woodworkers Store, Rogers, MN; Tool Trend Ltd., Concord, Ont.; Unicorn Abrasives of Canada, Brockville, Ont.; Veritas Tools Inc., Ottawa Ont./Ogdensburg, NY; Woodcraft Supply Corp., Parkersburg, WV

SHARPENING AND MAINTAINING HAND TOOLS
Adjustable Clamp Co., Chicago, IL; Anglo-American Enterprises Corp., Somerdale, NJ; Black and Decker/Elu Power Tools, Hunt Valley, MD; Cooper Tools, Apex, NC; Delta International Machinery/Porter Cable, Guelph, Ont.; Diamond Machinery Technology Inc., Marlborough, MA; Garrett Wade Company, New York, NY; General Tools Manufacturing Co., New York, NY; Great Neck Saw Mfrs. Inc. (Buck Bros. Division), Millbury, MA; Lee Valley Tools Ltd., Ottawa, Ont.; Norton Abrasives Canada Inc., Montreal, Que.; Record Tools Inc., Pickering, Ont.; Robert Sorby Ltd., Sheffield, U.K./Busy Bee Machine Tools, Concord, Ont.; Sandvik Saws and Tools Co., Scranton, PA; The Woodworkers Store, Rogers, MN; Veritas Tools Inc., Ottawa Ont./Ogdensburg, NY; Woodcraft Supply Corp., Parkersburg, WV

SHARPENING POWER TOOL BLADES AND BITS
Adjustable Clamp Co., Chicago, IL; Adwood Corp., High Point, NC; Anglo-American Enterprises Corp., Somerdale, NJ; Black and Decker/Elu Power Tools, Hunt Valley, MD; Cooper Tools, Apex, NC; Delta International Machinery/Porter Cable, Guelph, Ont.; Diamond Machinery Technology Inc., Marlborough, MA; Garrett Wade Company, New York, NY; General Tools Manufacturing Co., New York, NY; Great Neck Saw Mfrs. Inc. (Buck Bros. Division), Millbury, MA; Hitachi Power Tools U.S.A. Ltd., Norcross, GA; Laguna Tools, Laguna Beach, CA; Lee Valley Tools Ltd., Ottawa, Ont.; Norton Abrasives Canada Inc., Montreal, Que.; Record Tools Inc., Pickering, Ont.; Sandvik Saws and Tools Co., Scranton, PA; The Woodworkers Store, Rogers, MN; Tool Trend Ltd., Concord, Ont.; Veritas Tools Inc., Ottawa Ont./Ogdensburg, NY; Woodcraft Supply Corp., Parkersburg, WV; Woodstock International, Bellingham, WA; Wood Systems Inc., New Berlin, WI

MAINTAINING PORTABLE POWER TOOLS
Adjustable Clamp Co., Chicago, IL; Black and Decker/Elu Power Tools, Hunt Valley, MD; Delta International Machinery/Porter Cable, Guelph, Ont.; Dewalt Industrial Tool Co., Hampstead, MD; General Tools Manufacturing Co., Inc., New York, NY; Hitachi Power Tools U.S.A. Ltd., Norcross, GA; Lee Valley Tools Ltd., Ottawa, Ont.; Newman Tools Inc., Montreal, Que; Sears, Roebuck and Co., Chicago, IL; Stanley Tools, Division of the Stanley Works, New Britain, CT; Steiner-Lamello A.G Switzerland/Colonial Saw Co., Kingston, MA; Tool Trend Ltd., Concord, Ont.

MAINTAINING STATIONARY POWER TOOLS
Adjustable Clamp Co., Chicago, IL; Campbell Hausfeld, Harrison, OH; Cooper Tools, Apex, NC; Delta International Machinery/Porter Cable, Guelph, Ont.; General Tools Manufacturing Co., Inc., New York, NY; Hitachi Power Tools U.S.A. Ltd., Norcross, GA; Jet Equipment and Tools, Auburn, WA; Newman Tools Inc., Montreal, Que; Sears, Roebuck and Co., Chicago, IL; Stanley Tools, Division of the Stanley Works, New Britain, CT; Vermont American Corp., Lincolnton, NC and Louisville, KY

The following persons also assisted in the preparation of this book:
Lorraine Doré, Graphor Consultation, Solange Laberge, Rob Lutes, Geneviève Monette

PICTURE CREDITS

Cover Robert Chartier
6,7 Marie Louise Duruaz
8,9 Steve Lewis
10,11 Perry Zavitz
14 *(lower left, lower right)* Hans Blohm